Trump, The Warrior

Son of A Late Muslim League Leader Speaks

Shahinul Khalisdar, EA, MST

Dedication

I have dedicated this book to my beloved father, who has struggled all his life to make Muslim life better by sacrificing his comfort zone, a legacy he inherited from his father, Muhammed Masim Khalisdar. This man dreamt of a peaceful, prosperous, and militarily Muslim solid country, United Pakistan 1947-1971, East Pakistan 1955-1971 (Bangladesh 1971-present), and West Pakistan 1947-1971, so no colonialists ever dared to enslave the Muslims again.

Contents

Dedication iii

Preface vii

Introduction 1

The USA And The Americans 5

Illegal immigrant 14

My Migration Story 17

Muslim 22

I And The Political USA 32

The USA Government 37

Domestic Policy 39

Crime In The USA 47

Justice in the USA 54

Defund The Police 56

In Islamic History, The Police 63

Military Coup 65

Sex Politics 68

Women Rights 74

Racial Politics 78

Voter Fraud 82

2020 Election Drama 85

The January 6th 96

Donald Trump's Sexual Misconduct Allegations 111

Why does the establishment hate Trump? 116

America's New Saver Nikki Haley 118

U.S. Primary 2024 121

The USA Foreign Policy 124

Peace through strength......................................127

September 11th And A War On Terror 130

Islamic Terrorists..134

Afghanistan Withdrawal......................................141

Biden Admin Has 'Undermined' Israel. 145

Antisemitism Exposed (Fox News) 148

Muslim and American Relationship 153

The USA Is the World Leader 158

Third World War 161

Conclusion 164

References...169

About The Author...172

Preface

This book is a culmination of my reflections on former President Donald Trump, drawn from the hundreds of comments I wrote on his 2015-2019 official Facebook Page, Twitter, and various social media platforms. These comments were not just observations but reflections of my personal experiences and interactions with the political landscape.

As a Tax Advisor, small businessman, and community worker, I have always been mindful of the potential impact of my political views on my clients and community service. Recognizing the diversity of opinions and speculations about each other, I have chosen to tread carefully and previously refrain from making political comments, a decision I believed to be wise and respectful.

Since Former President Donald Trump announced his presidential candidacy in 2015, I wrote daily on his Facebook page, believing in this Hadith that the Prophet (ﷺ) said, "The deen (religion) is naseehah (advice)." We said, "To whom?" He (ﷺ) said, "To Allah, His Book, His Messenger, and to the leaders of the Muslims and their common folk." [Muslim]

Of course, presidential candidate Donald Trump was not a Muslim leader or a political leader, but I believed he could win the election. Furthermore, he will become the leader of the pro-religious and free-market world. Obviously, I was quite disappointed with his policies.

However, I was incredibly thankful to his Facebook admin team. My comments used to go against FaxeBook's community standards policy more than hundreds of times, and Facebook removed some of the comments. Still, Mr. Trump's Facebook admin team never blocked me or removed my comment from the page; instead, they filtered the abusive language in my comments from others. In contrast, Presidential Candidate Hillary Clinton's team removed my comments from her official Facebook Page. Finally, I closed my previous Facebook account in 2019.

I thought of writing a book on the USA after the September 11, 2001, heinous attacks on the Twin Towers. As the 20th anniversary of September 11 passed, I thought it was about time to complete the book. I had done it by rewriting the Facebook comment written on the Former President's Facebook page:

"Trump the Warrior" is a unique characteristic book. I would like you all who desire to hear from the traditional Muslim political side of the story to please spread word of mouth.

I am also thankful to my dear, lovely father, who raised me in his old age and taught me world politics, economy, society, writing, and reading with care and love. Michele Parker, Ph.D., allowed me to finish my 11th and 12th-grade high school equivalence at BMCC without attending any school in my life in the past.

Introduction

I have been living in the USA for over three decades. As I learned, risking everything for a chance at a better life, many illegal immigrants seek a new home in America, which means dangerous journeys by water. With stricter enforcement on land, record numbers of migrants are attempting dangerous ocean crossings. The border with Mexico extends far beyond the desert, river, and ocean. Those who are brave enough to cross the border and the open waters face an uncertain future in the USA.

As I witnessed, many people risk their lives to come to the USA for a better life because they believe that making money here is easy. But my point in writing this book is about the US policies and political culture, which President Trump contradicts, not about the sympathetic illegal immigrants' stories.

As USA foreign policy is concerned, the USA is at war with Muslims in the name of radical Islam and Islamic terrorists. The War on Terror, declared by George Bush, is a military campaign started by the U S after the September 11 attacks. Its primary targets are militant Islamist groups such as Al-Qaeda, the Taliban, and their allies. The campaign has spanned multiple wars and conflicts, including the invasion of Iraq in 2003 to depose the Ba'athist regime and fight various militant factions during the ensuing insurgency. The Islamic State militia has also emerged as a key adversary of the United States after its territorial expansion in 2014.

The reason I desired to write Trump the Warrior is that the US media painted Islam as a religion of terrorist manufacturers without telling the truth. With federal government support, the FBI orchestrated sting operations on the ground. NYC Mayor Bloomberg orchestrated systematic Muslim harassment by using NYPD Hispanics, or maybe Hispanics took advantage of Bloomberg's anti-Muslim policy, which empowered Mr. Trump to declare a "Muslim Ban" publicly.

On the other hand, the FBI orchestrated sting operations in the Muslim community Masjid to Masjid by using informants. Some of the informants, to please the FBI, unnecessarily played tricky games with the emotionally angry Muslims to trap them into being provocative, giving them an excuse to arrest them and portray them as terrorists to build their credibility. Because of their deceptive games, the FBI arrested a few dozen innocent Muslims only because they had expressed their anger and distasteful opinions to the FBI informant regarding the USA foreign policy.

Still, the US media portrays the entire Muslim population as a united community to kill all the American infidels. It was a notorious crisis to be witnessed in my life as a grandson of a Muslim League founding member and son of a late Muslim

League leader. I was perplexed.

On the one hand, fourteen hundred years ago, the Messenger of Allah (ﷺ) predicted that Muslims would be divided into seventy-three sects. He (ﷺ) said: "Beware! The people of the Book (Jews and Christians) before were split up into seventy-two sects. This community (Muslim) will be split into seventy-three: seventy-two of them will go to Hell, and one of them will go to Paradise, and it is the majority group."

In my times, Muslims are deeply divided in political ideologies such as communism, socialism, secularism, democracy, republicanism, and political Islam. Also, Muslim countries created a mainstream culture of corruption and a subculture of religiously ignorant Mullah.

On the other hand, the US federal and local governments created a policy to target Muslims randomly and detain them systematically. At the same time, the media fueled the hatred against Muslims in the masses by using phrases like "Islamic Terrorists" and "Radical Islam."

What exactly can I do? Some people advised me to pen down so that people may understand the situation. I have been writing on the former president's Facebook page since 2015.

When it comes to writing a book, it can be challenging to decide on the intended audience. Some prefer flattery, while others want entertainment. However, for those seeking truth and insight, a comprehensive and straightforward approach is necessary. Our understanding of the world varies from person to person and culture to culture. Still, respecting one another is human dignity we can learn from each other, which is essential for a socially peaceful society.

Authoring a book based on personal experience, facts, policy, and expert opinions ensures that the truth is out there, even if it is not commercially successful. As the grandson of a Muslim League founding member and son of a late Muslim League leader, I understand the importance of standing by the truth. Let us revolutionize the facts and defeat all the lies.

The USA And The Americans

First of all, let me briefly tell you about America or the USA; otherwise, some of you may assume that I need to learn about the USA. The United States of America, commonly called "USA" or America, is primarily North America. It became independent on July 4th, 1776, from British colonialism. The USA consists of fifty states, a federal district, five major unincorporated territories, three hundred twenty-six Indian reservations, and some minor possessions. It is the world's fourth-largest country at 3.8 million square miles. The United States shares mainland borders with Canada to the north and Mexico to the south and has limited maritime borders with Cuba, Russia, and the Bahamas. With more than 331 million people living in the USA, it is the third most populous country in the world. The national capital is Washington, DC, and the most populous city is New York City.

The World assumes that the "White" (Europeans) people are Americans. According to US law, any individual who is a US citizen is recognized as an American. In my understanding, there are three types of US citizens: natural-born, foreign-born, and naturalized. The natural-born is a person born within the USA's jurisdiction. A foreign-born US citizen is a person whose parents are US citizens but who resided in a foreign country while giving birth to that person or a foreign woman married to a US citizen who gave birth in a foreign country; that person is a foreign-born US citizen. A naturalized USA citizen is a person who has lived in the USA as a legal resident for at least five years, has applied for citizenship, has taken a citizenship test, and has taken an oath to be a US citizen.

As I have observed, based on the stereotype, only the "White (Europeans) people are considered American." Some people will never believe you are an American if you are not a "White" American and are not born in the USA. The foreign immigration authorities and the USA Border Guard may frequently challenge you.

However, from my understanding, there are four types of Americans: Native Americans or Indians, Early Settlers, Repatriation Americans and Immigrant Americans.

Native Americans

Native Americans or Indians. According to historians' expert opinion, Paleo-Indians migrated from Siberia to the American continent at least twelve thousand years ago; these people are called "Native," "Indigenous," or "Indians." They mostly live in Indian reservations, a designated area allocated by the federal government for them.

Early Settlers

The Early Settlers from British colonization began in the 16th century along the East Coast of the New World. The United States materialized from the thirteen British colonies and early settlers along the East Coast. Their disputes over taxation and political representation with Great Britain led to the creation of the Union States. The American Revolutionary War (1775–1783) established an independent country, the USA; these people were called early settlers. They are founding US citizens and the first to be politically recognized as Americans.

Repatriated Americans

*"I am naturally anti-slavery. If slavery is not wrong, nothing is wrong," - **President Abraham Lincoln.***

In the late 18th century, Repatriated Americans in the U.S. began growing across North America and were colonized by Europeans such as France, Spain, and Britain. The USA gained control of new territories in the south and west, sometimes through war, political settlement, and purchasing.

In 1848, slavery was legal in the southern newly admitted states in the USA until the second half of the 19th century when the USA Civil War broke out from April 12th, 1861, to May 9th, 1865. In 1965, the Federal Government officially abolished slavery and ended the Civil War.

In the Spanish–American War in 1919, the USA defeated

the Spanish colonial masters, most in North America except Mexico; the United States extended over the continent Atlantic to the Pacific oceans; these all are repatriated Americans.

Sadly, most black people believe they are still treated as second-class citizens and are reluctant to integrate with mainstream American society. Nevertheless, the USA bears the burden of mass killing and displacing Native Americans to acquire more Union territories.

Immigrants Americans

"The USA is a Nation of Immigrants" - **John F. Kennedy**

Immigrant Americans played a crucial role in the USA's intellectual, scientific and economic development known as the Industrial Revolution. They did not migrate to the USA as slaves or British settlers. They immigrated to the USA of their free will to avoid political problems and persecution for scientific theory, philosophical writings, analyzing publishing, and religious sectarian hostilities in their native lands.

The Naturalization Act of 1790 was a pick-and-choose immigration policy that Naturalized Citizenship to "free white (Europeans)"; it included blacks (Africans) in the 1860s and Asians in the 1950s as well. Historically, in the early years of the migration to the USA, yearly basis immigrants were fewer than 8,000, including French refugees from Haiti due to the slave revolt in 1791. Subsequently, in 1820, immigrants regularly poured into the USA because it was more welcoming to new immigrants due to industrialization demand for workers and inventors than Latin America.

The difference between the USA and Latin America was that the US founding fathers were British and protestant Christians. Latin America was Catholic and forced people to convert to Catholicism. That is why most migrants preferred the USA over Latin America. Most of the people were brought to Latin America from Muslim Andalusians. They were forcefully converted to Catholicism, and forty men raped one woman to erase their Muslim identity.

However, from 1836 to 1914, more than 30 million Western Europeans migrated to the United States because of constant conflict between countries and religious riots between Protestants and Catholics in Western Europe. The death rate of transatlantic during the journey to the USA was high due to poor ship conditions, food shortages, and rough weather, of which one in seven migrants died in that period.

In 1875, the US Congress passed its first immigration law, known as the Page Act of 1875. The wave of migrants coming from China resulted from the California Gold Rush. Congress passed an immigration law to ban Chinese from entering the USA, known as the Chinese Exclusion Act of 1882. The law was in effect until the law was repealed in 1943. In the late 1800s, immigration from some Asian countries became usual, especially to the West Coast of the USA. The peak year of European immigration was 1907, when 1,285,349 Europeans entered the USA. In 1910, according to the USA immigration statistics, more than 13 million Western European immigrants were living in the USA.

In 1921, an Emergency Quota Act was enacted, followed by the Immigration Act of 1924. The 1924 Act, reason behind this Act, was to restrict immigrants entering the USA from Southern and Eastern Europe, mainly Jewish, Italian, and Slavic people, fearing the spreading Communism and mafia activity in the USA, who had already begun to enter the USA in the early 1890s. Migration to the USA in the 1930s substantially declined due to the Great Depression from Western Europe. In the final year of the flourishing USA industrialization, only 279,678 immigrants in 1929 migrated to the USA on record. Nevertheless, then again, in 1933, only 23,068 emigrated to the U.S. from Europe.

In the early 1930s, more Americans migrated from the USA to foreign countries such as Germany than immigrated to the USA. The U.S. Government created a Mexican Repatriation program to encourage people to relocate to Mexico during those years voluntarily. However, contrary to the policy, the US government started deporting thousands of people against their will.

In recent days, the US foreign policy has been an unbreakable tie between Israel and the USA. Nevertheless, most Jewish were fleeing the Nazi persecution in World War II were banned from entering the United States. In the post-war era, the Justice Department launched Operation Wetback, under which 1,075,168 Mexicans were deported in 1954. About 400,000 Mexicans were repatriated to Mexico, and half of them were U.S. citizens.

The Immigration and Nationality Act of 1965 repealed the national-origin quotas system. By equalizing immigration policies, the Act resulted in new immigration from non-European countries, which changed the ethnic demographics of the United States. In 1970, 60% of immigrants were from Europe, which decreased to 15% by 2000. In the 2000s, the decline in migration from Europe significantly improved the Western European economy.

In 1990, President George H. W. Bush signed the Immigration Act of 1990, which increased legal immigration to the United States by 40%. In 1991, President Bush signed the Armed Forces Immigration Adjustment Act 1991, allowing foreign service members who had served 12 or more years in the U.S. Armed Forces to qualify for permanent residency and, in some cases, for Citizenship.

Lottery Immigration Visa Program

The Diversity Immigration Visa program, also known as the DV program, is an initiative by the United States government to bring more people from different parts of the world to the USA. Acted in 1990, the program aims to diversify the United States immigrant population by selecting applicants from countries with minimal numbers of immigrants in the USA in the last five years. Annually, the program makes available 55,000 immigrant visa applicants through a lottery program administered by the Department of State under the Immigration and Nationality Act.

The idea of diversifying immigration came during President Ronald Reagan's administration in 1986. A few temporary immigrant visa programs, such as family members or employment visas, were created outside the normal immigration visa process. The DV program is the third program, and it selects applicants from countries that had been "adversely affected" by prior immigration policies.

While the program has been successful in diversifying the immigrant population, some groups, such as undocumented illegal immigrants, continue to face challenges. As of today, more than eleven million undocumented illegal immigrants are in the USA, and most illegal women immigrants are victims of sex slavery and working in poor working conditions in the suburban Southern States of the USA.

The Diversity Visa Lottery Program, administered by the Department of State, offers a chance for 55,000 immigrant visa applicants to obtain permanent residency in the United States. The program, established in 1986, aims to diversify the immigrant population in the United States by selecting applicants from countries with minimal numbers of immigrants in the USA in the last five years.

The program has undergone several changes over the years, with the first few temporary immigrant visa programs being issued on a first-come, first-served basis. The later programs, such as OP-1 and AA-1, were designed to benefit countries with an insignificant immigrant population in the United States.

While Ireland and Northern Ireland excessively benefited from these programs, Latin American and Haitian illegal immigrants outnumbered the legal immigrants.

Illegal immigrant

According to the Pew Research Center, the illegal immigrant population in the United States reached 10.5 million in 2021, a modest increase over 2019 but nearly identical to 2017, according to new estimates from the Pew Research Center. The most common country of birth for illegal immigrants is Mexico. However, the population of illegal immigrants from Mexico dropped by 900,000 from 2017 to 2021 to 4.1 million. There were increases in illegal immigrants from nearly every other region of the world – Central America, the Caribbean, South America, Asia, Europe, and sub-Saharan Africa.

Among U.S. states, only Florida and Washington saw increases in their illegal immigrant populations, while California and Nevada saw decreases. In all other states, illegal immigrant populations were unchanged. As of 2021, the nation's 10.5 million illegal immigrants represented about 3% of the total U.S. population and 22% of the foreign-born population. These shares were among the lowest since the 1990s.

It is important to note that the new estimates do not reflect changes that have occurred since apprehensions and expulsions of migrants along the U.S.-Mexico border started increasing in March 2021. Migrant encounters at the border have since reached historic highs.

Between 2007 and 2021, the illegal immigrant population decreased by 1.75 million, or 14%. Meanwhile, the legal immigrant population grew by more than 8 million, a 29% increase, and the number of naturalized U.S. citizens grew by 49%. In 2021, naturalized citizens accounted for about half (49%) of all immigrants in the country.

As the number of illegal immigrants living in the U.S. remains below its peak of 12.2 million in 2007, it is clear that the origin countries for illegal immigrants have changed since the population peaked. Mexico accounted for 39% of the nation's illegal immigrants.

The total number of illegal immigrants in the U.S. from countries other than Mexico has increased. In 2021, this population was 6.4 million, up by 900,000 from 2017. The U.S. illegal immigrant populations from most world regions grew from 2017 to 2021. Almost every region in the world had a notable increase in the number of illegal immigrants in the U.S. from 2007 to 2021. The most significant increases were from Central America (240,000) and South and East Asia (180,000).

After Mexico, the countries of origin with the largest illegal immigrant populations in the U.S. in 2021 were El Salvador (800,000), India (725,000), Guatemala (700,000), and Honduras (525,000). There are three Central American countries, El

Salvador, Honduras and Guatemala, which represented 2.0 million illegal immigrants in the U.S. in 2021, nearly 20% of the total. The illegal immigrant population from the Northern Triangle grew by about 250,000 in 2017 and about 700,000 in 2007. Venezuela was the country of birth for 190,000 U.S. illegal immigrants in 2021. This population has grown from 130,000 in 2017 to 55,000 in 2007.

Among the countries with the most significant numbers of illegal immigrants in the U.S., India, Brazil, Canada, and former Soviet Union countries experienced growth from 2017 to 2021. The illegal immigrant populations remained the same, unchanged from China (375,000) and the Dominican Republic (230,000).

The number of illegal immigrants in the U.S. workforce has remained steady since 2017. In 2021, the share of illegal immigrants in the U.S. workforce was slightly less than 5%, compared with 3% of the total U.S. population. It is interesting to note that the illegal immigrant population includes relatively few children or elderly adults, groups that tend not to be in the labor force. In 2021, about 7.8 million illegal immigrants were in the U.S. labor force. This was up slightly from 2019 but smaller than every year from 2007 through 2015. (Note:- there is no authentic research conducted from 2021 to 24)

My Migration Story

I heard from my maternal grandfather, Arshad Ali Chaudhry, who used to work on a ship. I heard from him that his ship docked at the Port of Baltimore in 1939. He told me lots of stories about Baltimore and Maryland; Baltimore is a city inside of the state of Maryland. Maryland is a land filled with tall trees that do not produce fruits. According to my understanding, he was comparing Maryland with his village, K.M. Tilla; it is a fertile land. All kinds of fruits grow, plus rice. He always disliked the USA. After finishing his ship's job, he returned to his beloved village and died there in 2000. He never returns to the USA after 1970.

My maternal older uncle came to the USA as my grandfather's older son and started working in the ship's company. My uncle applied for all of his sisters to bring them to the USA against my grandfather's will. My grandfather wanted us to stay in K.M. Tilla in-house and take care of his lands, but everyone decided to come to the USA.

I never knew who was right, my dad or my maternal grandfather. My dad wanted us to be in the USA because Bangladesh has an uncertain future and is politically unstable. Both of them had two points of view.

As I was born into the upper class, I can see everything

crystal clear now. The problem is not with the countries. The problem is that envy and jealousy create a vicious caste and class system and racial discrimination in the hearts and minds of the people. Any country can be a good country if all its citizens take civic duty as its core principle.

Why do you support the Muslim ban in the USA and Western Europe?

Over the years, many people have asked me, "Why do you support the Muslim ban?" To answer this question, I would like the reader to know that, first and foremost, we all are human beings, as the Quran mentioned, "O mankind! Indeed, We have created you from a male and a female and made you into nations and tribes so that you may get to know one another. Surely, the noblest of you in the sight of Allah is the most righteous among you. Allah is truly All-Knowing, All-Aware." (49:13)

Firstly, readers need to understand that I am the grandson of a Muslim League founding member and the son of a Muslim League leader. My primary objective is to look into Muslim interests, and I intend to give an opinion that will benefit Muslims. In any situation, I will not compromise Muslim interests.

Secondly, Lord Curzon advised the Muslim upper class in 1898 to form a political party instead of violence in Bengal. The Muslim League was created in 1906. Muslim League's primary objective was to liberate Muslims from Hindu Raja and Zamindars' Proza (Slavery).

Muslim League built Dhaka University in 1921 in cooperation with the British Government in the belief that Muslims would learn English, Mathematics, Chemistry, the Quran with understanding and many other vital subjects. Dhaka University turned out to be a vicious enemy of Muslims, a center for hardcore Bengali nationalism and Communist movements.

Muslim League created Pakistan on the basis of the two-nation theory to have an example state that will be prosperous and economically sound, and the youth will be educated and militarily strong country. Instead, we are witnessing it as a bankrupt, religiously ignorant, and earned the nicknames "Failed State," Beggar State," "Whore", "Terrorist Exporter," "beggar exporter," and "Mother of religious sectarian violence."

East Pakistan's name changed to Bangladesh, and Bengali dance on Muslim dead bodies. The reason Muslim leaders in 1900 agreed with Lord Curzon and President Roosevelt in the 1940s to send Muslims to the U.K. and USA was to educate Muslims in engineering, architecture, medical science, and military training, which were absent in the Muslim community due to colonialism, not for economic migrants.

The Muslim living standard in Western Europe and the

USA is worse than Hindu Dalits in India. Characteristically, they are categorized as street criminals. They are not demonstrating Islamic principles and values, which may give a positive thought about Muslims; instead, they are a threat to civil society and a total embarrassment to Islam. They should live in their native land. Eventually, they may realize that they have to learn Islamic monotheism and take individual responsibility to change society gradually.

Donald Trump's anti-immigration Stance

Donald Trump is doubling down on his anti-immigration policies, promising to carry out mass deportations and establish deportation camps along the border if he is re-elected. Trump claims that countries are "emptying their prisons" into the U.S. and that his crackdowns would send shock waves to all the world's criminal smugglers.

Critics have called his plans "dangerous" and "dehumanizing," with some likening them to a "20th-century dictator's playbook." Meanwhile, Trump's allies argue that the problem is on an "industrial scale" and that drastic measures are necessary. With the election just weeks away, immigration continues to be a divisive issue that both parties are using to rally their bases.

Mr. Trump said that countries are "emptying their prisons"

into the U.S. I could not agree more. I have seen a few criminals from my native city of Sylhet, Bangladesh, on the NYC Subway in the late 1990s. I was shocked at how they came to the USA. We had to go through a vetting process, but how these criminals came to the USA, and then I learned that they had crossed the Mexico border.

Muslim

I feel it is essential for the readers to know about Muslims. The USA spent trillions of dollars fighting against Muslims, calling them "Muslim Fundamentalists." Also, Western colonial powers fought against Muslims for nearly three hundred years during colonialism.

Muslims are known as monotheistic religious people or one of the Abrahamic religions. Muslims are those who practice Islam. the Messenger of Allah (ﷺ) said, "Islam has built on five [pillars]: testifying that there is nothing worthy of worship except Only One God and that Prophet Muhammad is the Messenger of Allah, establishing (five times) the salah (prayer), paying the zakat (obligatory charity), making the hajj (pilgrimage) to the Makkah, and fasting in the month of Ramadhan." [Bukhari & Muslim]

Islam is different from Hindu or Buddhist scholars who debate on historical counts and archaeological evidence to prove its authenticity. Islam is a monotheistic religion. Its knowledge derives from two authentic sources, the Quran and authentic hadiths, unlike any other historical study. In Islam, historical counts are very different from any other religion in the World. For example, Muslims do not believe that humans randomly evolved from apes. Human beings' lives began with creating two people, a male and a female, named Adam and Hawwa (Eve).

Fundamentally, Muslims believe Allah created Adam with His hand, breathed into him his soul created by Him, and told His angels to prostrate to him. Allah created Adam from dust, as He says, "Verily, the likeness of 'Eesa (Jesus) before Allah is the likeness of Adam. He created him from dust, then (He) said to him: 'Be!' — and he was ' [3:59]. When Allah had completed the creation of Adam, He commanded the angels to prostrate to him, so they prostrated, except for Iblees (Devil), who was present, but he refused and was too arrogant to prostrate to Adam. "(Remember) when your Lord said to the angels: 'Truly, I am going to create man from clay. So when I have fashioned him and breathed into him (his) soul created by Me, then you fall down on prostrate to him.' So the angels prostrated themselves, all of them, Except for Iblees (Devil), he was proud and was one of the disbelievers" [38:71-74]. Then Allah told the angels that He was going to place Adam on earth and make generations after generations of his offspring, as He said, "And (remember) when your Lord said to the angels: 'Verily, I am going to place (mankind) generations after generations on earth'" [2:30] Allah taught Adam all the names: "And He taught Adam all the names (of everything)" [2:31]

When Iblees (Devil) refused to prostrate Adam, Allah expelled him from heaven and cursed him: "(Allah) said: 'Then get out from here; for verily, you are outcast. And verily, My Curse is on you till the Day of Recompense'" [38:77-78] When Iblees (Devil) knew of his fate, he asked Allah to give him respite until the Day of Resurrection: "[Iblees (Devil)] said: 'My Lord! Give me then respite till the day the (dead) are resurrected.' (Allah) said: 'Verily, you are of those allowed respite Till the Day of the time appointed'" [38:79-81] When Allah granted him that, he declared war on Adam and his descendants, made disobedience attractive to them and tempted them to commit immoral actions: "[Iblees (Devil)] said: 'By Your Might, then I will surely, mislead them all, Except Your chosen slaves amongst them (i.e., faithful, obedient, true believers of Islamic Monotheism).'" [38:82-83] Allah created Adam, and from him, He created his wife. From their progeny, He created men and women, as He says, "O mankind! Be dutiful to your Lord, Who created you from a single person (Adam), and from him (Adam) He created his wife [Hawwa (Eve)], and from them both He created many men and women" [4:1]

Then Allah caused Adam and his wife to dwell in Paradise as a test for them. He commanded them to eat of the fruits of Paradise, but He forbade them to eat from one tree: "And We said: 'O Adam! Dwell you and your wife in the Paradise and eat both of you freely with pleasure and delight, of things therein as wherever you will, but come not near this tree or you both will be of the Zalimoon (wrong-doers)'"

Allah warned Adam and his wife against the Devil, as He

said, "O Adam! Verily, this is an enemy to you and your wife. So let him not get you both out of Paradise so that you will be distressed." [20:117] The Devil whispered to Adam and his wife and tempted them to eat from the forbidden tree. Adam forgot and could not resist the temptation, so he disobeyed his Lord and ate from that tree: "Then Devil whispered to him, saying: 'O Adam! Shall I lead you to the Tree of Eternity and to a kingdom that will never waste away?'

Then they both ate of the tree, so their private parts became manifest to them, and they began to cover themselves with the Paradise leaves for their covering. Thus did Adam disobey his Lord, so he went astray." [20:120-121] Their Lord called to them and said, "Did I not forbid you that tree and tell you: Verily, Devil is an open enemy unto you?" [7:22]

When they ate from the tree, they regretted their actions and said: "Our Lord! We have wronged ourselves. If You forgive us not and bestow not upon us Your Mercy, we shall certainly be of the losers." [7:23]

The sin of Adam stemmed from desire, not from arrogance; hence, Allah guided him to repent, and He accepted that from him: "Then Adam received from his Lord Words. And his Lord pardoned him (accepted his repentance). Verily, He is the One Who forgives (accepts repentance), the Most Merciful." [2:37]

Repent is the way for Adam and his descendants: whoever sins then regrets sincerely, Allaah will accept his repentance: "And He is Who accepts repentance from His slaves, and forgives sins, and He knows what you do"[42:25] Then Allah sent Adam and his wife, and Iblees (Devil), down to the earth, and He sent down Revelation to them, and He sent the Messengers to them. So whoever believes will enter Paradise and whoever disbelieves will enter Hell: "We said: 'Get down all of you from this place (the Paradise), then whenever there comes to you Guidance from Me, and whoever follows My Guidance, there shall be no fear on them, nor shall they grieve. But those who disbelieve and believe Our Ayaat (proofs, evidence, verses, lessons, signs, revelations.) — such are the dwellers of the fire. They shall abide therein forever." [2:38-39]

When Allah sent them all down to the earth, the conflict between faith and disbelief, truth and falsehood, and good and evil began. It will continue until Allah inherits the World and everyone in it: "(Allah) said: 'Get down, one of you an enemy to the other [i.e., Adam, Hawwa, (Eve), and Iblees (Devil)]. On earth will be a dwelling place for you and an enjoyment for a time.' [7:24]

Allah can do all things. He created Adam with no father or mother, and He created Hawwa from a father with no mother, and He created 'Eesa from a mother with no father, and He created us from a father and a mother. Allah created Adam from dust, then

He made his descendants from semen of despised water, as He says (interpretation of the meaning): "Who made everything He has created good, and He began the creation of man from clay.

Then, He made his offspring from semen of despised water (male and female sexual discharge). Then He fashioned him in due proportion and breathed into him the soul (created by Allah for that person), and He gave you hearing (ears), sight (eyes), and hearts. Little is the thanks you give!" [32:7-9]

How man is created in the womb and the stages he goes through are wondrous. Allah mentioned this in the Quran: "And indeed, We created man (Adam) out of an extract of clay (water and earth). After that, We made him (the offspring of Adam) as a Nutfah (mixed drops of the male and female sexual discharge and lodged it) in a safe lodging (womb of the woman). Then We made the Nutfah into a clot (a piece of thick coagulated blood), then We made the clot into a little lump of flesh, then We made out of that little lump of flesh bones, then We clothed the bones with flesh, and then We brought it forth as another creation. So Blessed is Allah, the Best of creation." [23:12-14]

Allah Alone creates whatever He wills. He knows what is in the wombs, and He decrees provision and lifespans (for His creatures): "To Allah belongs the Kingdom of the heavens and the earth. He creates what He wills. He bestows females (offspring) upon whom He wills, and He bestows males (offspring) upon whom He wills. He bestows both males and females, and He renders barren whom He wills. Verily, He is the All-Knower and can do all things." [42:49-50]

The Prophet (PBUH) said: "Allah has appointed an angel over the womb. He says, 'O Lord, a drop of semen (nutfah); O Lord, a clot ('alaqah); O Lord, a little lump of flesh (mudghah).' Then, if Allah wishes (to complete) its creation, the angel asks, (O Lord) male or female, wretched (doomed to Hell) or blessed (destined for Paradise)? How much will his provision be? And what will his lifespan be?' So that is written while (the child) is still in the mother's womb." (Narrated by al-Bukhaari, 318)

"See you not (O men) that Allah has subjected for you whatsoever is in the heavens and whatsoever is in the earth, and has completed and perfected His Graces upon you, (both) apparent (i.e., Islamic Monotheism, and the lawful pleasures of this World, including health, good looks) and hidden [i.e., one's faith in Allah (of Islamic Monotheism), knowledge, wisdom, guidance for doing righteous deeds, and also the pleasures and delights of the Hereafter in Paradise] [31:20]

Allah has distinguished and honored man with reason by which he knows his Lord, Creator, and Provider, and by which he knows what is right and evil, what will benefit him and what will harm him, what is halaal and what is haraam. Allah did not create man and leave him alone with no path to follow. Instead, Allah revealed the Books and sent Messengers to guide humanity to the Straight Path.

Allah created people with a natural inclination towards Monotheism (Tawhid – belief in the Oneness of Allah). Allah sent a Prophet to bring them back to the Straight Path every time they deviated from that. The first of the Prophets was Adam, and the last was Muhammad (peace and blessings of Allah be upon him):

Mankind was one community, and Allah sent Prophets with glad tidings and warnings. With them, He sent down the Scripture in truth to judge between people in matters wherein they differed [2:213]. All the Messengers called people to the same fact, which is the worship of Allah alone and to reject all false gods besides Him: "And verily, We have sent among every Ummah (community, nation) a Messenger (proclaiming): "Worship Allah (Alone), and avoid (or keep away from) Taaghoot (all false deities, i.e., do not worship Taaghoot besides Allah)." [16:36]

The religion with which Allah sent the Prophets and Messengers was the same, i.e., Islam: "Truly, the religion with Allah is Islam." [3:19] The last of the heavenly Books which Allah revealed was the Qur'an, confirming the Books which came before it, and as a guide to all of mankind:

The last of the Prophets and Messengers whom Allah sent was Muhammad (peace and blessings of Allah be upon him): "Muhammad is not the father of any of your men, but he is the Messenger of Allah and the last (end) of the Prophets." [33:40] Allah sent Muhammad (peace and blessings of Allah be upon him) to all of mankind: "Say (O Muhammad): 'O mankind! Verily, I am sent to you all as the Messenger of Allah'" [7:158] [3:85]

The religion which was brought by Muhammad (PBUH) confirms the message conveyed by the Prophets before him, in its basic principles and advocation of noble characteristics, as Allah says, "He (Allah) has ordained for you of religion (Islamic Monotheism) what He ordained for Nooh (Noah), and that which We have revealed to you (O Muhammad), and that which We ordained for Ibraaheem (Abraham), Moosa (Moses) and 'Eesa (Jesus) saying you should establish the religion (i.e., to do what it orders you to do practically) and make no divisions] therein (religion, i.e., various sects in religion). [42:13]

Many of my non-Muslim college friends in the late 95s, Hindu, Christian, Jewish, and Shia, speculated that I was hiding something about Muslim beliefs from them to make myself more fitting with them. The above verses of the Quran can be verified or searched online. I have no reason to lie or fabricate the knowledge from any of Adam's children.

So Jesus said to the Jews who had believed him, "If you abide in my word, you are truly my disciples, and you will know the truth, and the truth will set you free." John 8:32

The Messenger of Allah (peace and blessings of Allah be upon him) said, "Those who came before you of the people of the book split into seventy-two sects, and this ummah will split into seventy-three sects. Seventy-two in Hell and one in Paradise, and that is the jama'ah (main body of Muslims)."

As we know, Prophet Muhammed (peace and blessings of Allah be upon him) predicted Muslims would be divided into seventy-three sects. It is better to adhere to the Quran and authentic Hadith to avoid religious tension among Muslims and non-Muslims alike.

{The above Quranic verses are interpreted meaning from Mushaf Usmani}

I And The Political USA

As a great-great-grandson son of Mirasdar, grandson of a Muslim League founding member, and son of a late Muslim League leader, I carry thousands of years of political DNA in my blood. On top of that, I learned politics on my father's lap. When I was a kid, I sat on my father's thigh almost every morning and leaned on his chest. That being said, I started hearing the political policies of the USA, UK, Soviet Union, India, and Pakistan at an early age.

There are significant differences between experienced politicians and new random politicians. Also, politicians were categorized throughout history as traditional patriotic, known as conservatives, who fought to maintain their traditional, social, political, religious, and regional values. The other group, known as the progressive, saw some societal issues and wanted to change them through a political settlement with the conservatives by negotiating the differences. Another group is known as opportunists; throughout history, their characters have been categorized as traitors, hypocrites, and flip-floppers, meaning they are not reliable on national interest. They only focus on their chair, nothing more.

For instance, a few months ago, I noticed my car had a weird noise. I went to a mechanic. He checked the car and told me,

"Brake pad and rotor gone." I asked him, "Can I change them in a few days or now." He said, "You can drive for a week." My mind did not agree with the mechanic. On the way, I asked a street mechanic about the car noise. He told me the same thing as the previous mechanic said: "The brake pad and rotor are gone."

In a couple of days, I went to a mechanic shop. I told the mechanic about the noise. He said, "Wait, let me call my boss." The main mechanic came. I told him about the noise. He looked at my face and asked me, "Can I have the car key?" I handed it to him. He drove inside the gas station for 30 sec.; he said: "your car arm is broken; you are lucky your car did not break down on the highway." He left. His assistant asked me, "Do you want to change it?" I replied, "Of course."

If we analyze this situation, we learn that it is "experience." All of them were mechanics. One checked the car with a torchlight and computer, and the other checked the exact vehicle with a light. But the one had experience. He checked nothing; he just heard the noise. By hearing the noise, he found out the exact problem in the car, which is called experience.

My personal experience is that the US media and lobbyists control the US's policies and elections. These two groups are controlled by well-trained mastermind foreign intelligence. Those "shadow" knows how to create a political mechanism to brainwash the nation. They focus on two elements, "minority" and "women." The minority has been an excellent political game for the last 70 years. Women have been a political game for over 100 years, sex has been a political game for 35 years, and Islamic terrorism has been a sexy Olympic game for over 300 years.

The Thirteen Colonies, also known as the "Thirteen British Colonies" or the "Thirteen American Colonies," were British colonies on the Atlantic coast of North America. They were established during the 17th and 18th centuries. The Thirteen Colonies later united the USA, which shared similar cultural, political, religious, and legal systems.

Protestant, Christian, and English-speaking people of British origin dominated the population. The Thirteen Colonies had a greater autonomous political status of self-governing and electorally elected officials to govern the colonies under the United Kingdom, not democratically elected officials. Later, they also resisted London's demands for more control over the colonies.

During 1754–1763, the French and Indian War against France and its Indian allies intensify tensions between Britain and the Thirteen Colonies. During the 1750s, the colonies began cooperating instead of directly contacting London for political issues. The inter-colonial cooperation created a sense of shared American identity between the Thirteen Colonies. They called for the protection of the colonists' "Rights as Englishmen," especially the demand of "no taxation without representation." They declared the independence of the USA on July 4th, 1776, forming a free and independent country from the Western European influence, the United States of America (USA).

On March 4th, 1789, the first Congress under the Constitution convened in New York City. On April 1st, 1789, Frederick Augustus Muhlenberg from Pennsylvania was chosen as the first Speaker of the House. On April 6th, 1789, George Washington was electorally elected the first President of the United States under the Constitution with 69 electoral votes, creating the first written "Constitutional Republic" in the world.

First, George Washington refused to become King after 15 years of warfare. He wanted to retire on his Potomac acres. At the request of many founding members of the USA, George Washington agreed to become a voluntary President. George Washington lost half of his wealth during the Revolutionary War and freed some slaves.

In the historical record, in 1774, George Washington publicly denounced the slave trade in the colonies on religious and moral grounds. After the Revolutionary War, he expressed his support for the abolition of slavery in the USA through a gradual legislative process, a view he shared widely. But in his private life, he had always used slaves and housemaids. He was dependent on slaves for his labor work.

Upon accepting the US presidency, George Washington refused to accept any payment for his eight years as commander in chief. President George Washington paid salaries to the newly hired administrative staff from his own wealth and eliminated more than five hundred Western European spies during the Presidency.

The USA Government

The United States is the first written "Constitutional Republic" in the World. However, almost all Americans believe the USA is a democratic country. The reason behind this is that the Democratic Party has been promoting the idea of democracy contrary to the founding fathers' structured political system for two hundred years. The founding fathers structured three branches of the governmental system and prevented commoners from voting to elect representatives. Only adult men of socially respected European descent, mainly of British origin, were allowed to vote.

The US governmental system was created as a written "Constitutional Republic," with a unique administrative governmental system formed as a federal government. The difference between the centralized and federal government systems is that the federal government would not directly impose authority over the Union States like a King or Emperor as the old World used to do. A centralized government can impose central control over the Union States like a King or Emperor.

The federal government was created with three separate governmental branches that will independently function within its constitutional rights. They are a democratically elected bicameral representative, Senate, and Congress, and an electorally elected president. The appointed judicial branch judges of government are confirmed by the Senate. Nevertheless, bicameral representatives, the USA Senates and Congress, and state governors are democratically elected; that is one reason most people perceive that the USA is a democratic country.

The "Constitutional Republic" USA has fifty autonomous states. The governor is the chief executive officer democratically elected as a governor at the state level. Also, every state has a judicial branch and a legislative branch. Similar to the Federal Government, the legislature is democratically elected, and judicial branch judges are appointed or elected depending on the state's legal framework.

My educated guess is that the USA's founding fathers got the governmental idea from the Islamic system of government. According to Sharia (Islamic Law), the governmental system is Khalifa's main federal administrative capacity and the Chief of Command. Khalifate falls in the "wa ulil amri minkum" category, meaning every Muslim must listen and obey as long as the Khalifa does not commit Shirk or Kufur. The Khalifate Governmental System is divided into three branches: No.1: Khalifa (Chief Executive and Chief of Command), No.2: Majlis-ash-Shura (consulting body), and No. 3: Sharia. Sharia is a judicial system. The Khalifa appoints a chief mufti as the final say on the judicial matter. All the Qadi (judges) are independently qualified to judge except for issuing Fatwa.

Domestic Policy

The expression "Domestic Policy" meant the plans and actions taken by the Federal Government on how to deal with domestic issues and needs to solve the problems within the country itself. The US Constitution precisely laid the domestic policy foundation for the Federal Governmental responsibilities as the Constitution's preamble stated: "We the People of the United States, in order to form a perfect Union, establish Justice, insure domestic Tranquility, provide for the common defense, promote the general Welfare, and secure the Blessings of Liberty to ourselves and our Posterity, do ordain and establish this Constitution for the United States of America."

The primary purpose of establishing the "Constitutional Republic" is to:

A. Establish justice,

B. Ensure domestic tranquility.

C. Provide for the common defense.

D. Promote the general welfare

E. Secure the blessings of liberty to ourselves and our posterity.

Let us analyze the five principles of fundamentally organizing and creating the Union, with a written "Constitution" as the guiding governing principle.

A. Establish justice: as the founding fathers of the USA fought against the imperial masters' injustices, they felt it was crucial to prioritize the "Justice System." The "Constitution" is crystal clear to create the "Supreme Court." The Constitution made the Supreme Court one of the separate branches of the government. On the main gate of "The Supreme Court" is written, "EQUAL JUSTICE UNDER LAW." It means that when all the judges walk into the courthouse, it is a reminder for them that "EQUAL JUSTICE UNDER LAW." Under all circumstances, the Judges must be biased, prejudiced, envious, jealous, hateful, and discriminatory thinking-free before entering the courthouse. As a former criminal justice student, I do not think that happens in the USA.

B. Ensure domestic tranquility: the founding fathers of European descent understood that the community's chronic domestic and social disturbance is not a healthy social environment. In Europe, ongoing religious intolerance, social injustices, and political fighting were ongoing phenomenal. That is why Europe could not intellectually, scientifically, politically, and socially advance itself. They wanted to create a peaceful society in the USA for those reasons. Making The Constitution a guiding principle, the politicians should be mindful of the "Domestic

Tranquility."

C. Provide for the common defense: Protecting the union's political boundary from external enemies and internal enemies is a sacred duty laid on the Federal Government, not going to foreign countries to bomb them. The military and militia must be used only for defending the USA.

D. Promote the general welfare: Instead of promoting the general welfare, the politicians promote the vice in society and create a toxic social discord among US citizens. As history witnesses, the USA's founding fathers were priests, landlords, traders, and journalists. They might have never thought that the politicians would have debated on homosexuality or sex in the USA. They would have felt inappropriate and offensive, and the founding fathers were of European descent. Europeans built a Christian religious culture for more than thousands of years before the USA was formed.

E. My educated guess is that their "General Welfare" meant charity work, helping needy families, building water supplies, roads, bridges, schools, Churches, and many other social good deeds. Most politicians do not read and understand the Constitution. They take an oath at the inauguration ceremony.

F. Secure the blessings of liberty to ourselves and our

posterity: This is a vital point in the USA. As founding fathers were of European descent, they knew pretty well how a king sent soldiers to arrest, execute, draft, exile, or randomly search people without justifiable cause. That is why they wanted to make sure that the US politicians understood the concept of "secure the Blessings of Liberty to ourselves and our Posterity."

In the USA, the Constitution guaranteed five freedoms: speech, religion, press, assembly, and the right to petition the government. I think that almost all Americans misunderstood the five freedoms because they lacked historical knowledge and were intellectually incapacitated to comprehend.

1. Freedom of Speech: This means a citizen can give a speech against the government or politicians without fearing imprisonment or beheading by the government. Historically, in Europe, people were beheaded for giving anti-governmental speeches or imprisoned for life. Most Americans believe that using obscene language is freedom of speech and liberty. When the founding fathers drafted and wrote the Constitution, obscene language was considered inappropriate and socially unacceptable.

2. Freedom of Religion: the "Freedom of Religion" was a critical essence of forming the Union. As we know, the founding fathers were of European descent, primarily of

British origin. They knew how important it is to have "Freedom of Religion." Europe was in a bloodbath for centuries in the name of religion. Protestants, Catholics, and Muslims have been fighting against each other for hundreds of years in Europe. As a Muslim living in NYC, I wholeheartedly felt how people survived in the dark age. Islam made the "Freedom of Religion" fourteen hundred years ago. "there is no compulsion" in religion. "Verily, the right path has become distinct from the wrong path" (2:256). Say: "O disbelievers! I worship not that which you worship. Nor will you worship whom I worship. And I shall not worship that which you are worshipping. Nor will you worship that which I worship. To you be your religion and to me my religion" (109:1-6).

3. Freedom of Press: In Europe, many people gave their lives, and their houses were burnt only because they wrote something criticizing the government or the Church. That is the specific reason the founding fathers felt it was crucial to constitutionally guarantee the right to write and publish without fear of governmental reprisal.

4. Freedom of Assembly: It was impossible to assemble during the 17th and 18th centuries in Europe and the Thirteen Colonies. Before the USA was formed, if people publicly assembled, the King assumed that there must be a

conspiracy to overthrow the government. Secretly assembled is considered a severe offense. Many people lost their lives only because they gathered to discuss specific issues. The Kings used to behead them publicly, unlike Islam. Islam allows public gatherings as the Quran states, " Invite to the way of your Lord with wisdom and fair preaching, and argue with them with that which is best. Indeed, your Lord best knows who has strayed from His path, and He best knows those who are guided. (16:125)". The founding fathers made it constitutionally legal to assemble without fearing governmental execution.

5. Freedom: "The right to petition the government." Best of my understanding, the USA is the first country on the face of the earth to give citizens "the right to petition the government constitutionally." However, in Muslim countries, the Muslim government used to appoint regional government representatives to listen to the people's concerns, unlike in Western Europe.

Historical fact shows that old politicians measured domestic policy based on Abrahamic religious doctrines with a moral consciousness. They grew up in the religious and social structure of the past. At present, politicians play games to win the crowd for the vote bank. I am confident that if these politicians were born in the eighteenth century, the USA would never have been formed, and this comprehensive constitution would never have been written and ratified.

However, sex, drugs, and money have become American culture since the nineteen-fifties. The average sexual partner in the USA is 7. Drugs are widely used to disregard socio-economic status. Politicians must realize that sex, drugs, and money are American realities. The cash flow must be in the economy to keep this country running stably.

Sex policing politics is not strategic domestic politics. Having multiple sexual partners is the social norm, and homosexuality is legal in the USA. Making laws to do sex policing will not solve anything except scaring the company in sex-related lawsuits. Sex law created a hot legal business but bankrupted and forced companies to outsource the jobs.

Girls are selling sex on F.B., Craigslist, dating apps, and many other types of apps. False sex complaints lead to billions of dollars wasted and cost millions of law enforcement paid hours. More than a million sex-related complaints and rape cases are still pending and unresolved. Sex is a socially accepted business; it is no longer counted for anti-social elements.

Using drugs is widely shared and costs billions of dollars to the local government to make drug-related arrests and prosecutions. Drug policing is no longer social welfare good politics.

At the cash, politicians have to have cash flow in the economy. The only option on the table is to print. That is the truth; otherwise, the country will face severe consequences.

The USA's domestic policy is no longer suitable for the "general welfare" concept. These days, Americans want a comfort zone and cash in the bank. If that fails, the government will face worse than January 6th.

Crime In The USA

As a former criminal justice student at Mercy College, I am well-educated in crime in the USA. But then again, the US media feel crimes in the USA are entertainment for recreational purposes only, not the governmental legal commitment to the citizens to deter crime to ensure the safety and security of the citizens.

Criminal law is vastly different from civil law. Civil law is part of a set of laws that is concerned with the private affairs of citizens, such as marriage, property ownership, and personal injuries, rather than with crime. Criminal Law is meant to deter severe offenses like robbery, murder, fraud and rape; criminal law is designed to punish those who commit such crimes, and it is nowhere near entertainment.

The objectives of criminal law are focused on retribution, deterrence, incapacitation, rehabilitation, and restoration.

Retribution, the goal is to punish the criminal for what they have done to others. It demands that criminals be punished without moral consideration because they have taken advantage of or inflicted harm on others. Criminal law will put the criminal at a "balance the scales."

Deterrence is aimed at discouraging offenders from criminal behavior, whether through individual or general deterrence.

Incapacitation is designed to keep criminals away from society, often achieved through prison sentences.

Rehabilitation aims to transform offenders into valuable members of society. At the same time, restoration is a victim-oriented theory of punishment that seeks to repair any injury inflicted on the victim by the offender. Understanding the objectives of criminal law is essential to ensuring that justice is served in the community.

However, the "constitution" precisely stated why the US government was formed on March 4, 1789. One of the pillars of the formation of the U.S. government is to ensure "justice." Still, the US media talk shows and moviemaking treat crime as entertainment, which is a good business for the film industry but seriously promotes vice in society and encourages teenagers to be influenced by it.

Sexualizing teenagers through movies, some call sex movies $100 billion worth of the "porn" industry. At the same time, it corrupts the young generation and teaches the young generation to treat girls without dignity like a sex commodity.

As a matter of fact, historically, crime has been an ancient anti-social element in society for millennia, which was identified as harmful to human beings. That is why every government is under oath to eliminate it.

Every crime is an antisocial element that harms human beings and victimizes citizens. In the past, for the most severe crimes, Capital punishments were imposed to deter repeated crimes in the community. Still, some states have it in place. Physical punishment, such as whipping and caning, was also imposed. As of today, these punishments are prohibited in many countries; instead, jail time is given.

In the USA, criminals are incarcerated in prison for a variety of jail times, including the death penalty, depending on the Federal, State and Local jurisdiction. The length of incarceration varies from a day to life imprisonment. Fines imposed, to some extent, seizing money or property from a person convicted of a crime.

Historically, a few millennia ago, to deter crime in the community, the cave, desert, and jungle habitats invented a new concept to ensure "justice for all" to deliver a peaceful society: "The Chieftain" or "Raja (Petty Kings)." The tribal Chieftains or regional kings (Rajas) were under oath to deliver justice. Still, they were financial slaves to the landlords because landlords used to pay taxes and send their children to help the chieftain or Raja defend the boundary from external enemies.

In the past, lords and traders supported the King or

Chieftain to protect their wealth, not out of love for the King or Chieftain. However, the Chieftain used public beheadings of criminals to show the public and to appease the community that they had iron fists against criminals. Many Chieftains or Kings were overthrown throughout history by Generals in the context of "restoration of law and order."

In recent history, many generals overthrew Prime Ministers or presidents' pretext of "restoration of law and order.". But, not a single one of them was ever to succeed in restoring law and order.

To deliver a peaceful society or country, thousand years ago, the Tribal Chieftain or Raja, landlords, and traders agreed to keep a judicial system independent and free from Landlords, traders, and the Chieftain or Raja's influence. However, the judicial system has often proven to be biased or partial.

A millennium ago, a judge's qualification was established based on merit and "intellectual capacity to distinguish right from wrong," which has been proven wrong in the USA.

The current judicial system abandoned the "common law. " It adopted the law enforcement theory, which made the judicial system a bureaucratic institution and a governmental puppet, not a judicial system independently serving the people on the criterion of "Right and Wrong."

In the USA, commonsense lawyering reasoning and facts

turned into three years of law school study. Of course, worldwide, the government has become a beyond-touch institution because Landlords no longer exist in societies. Corporations replace the landlords.

Contrary to "Right and Wrong," the U.S. Supreme Court website states that "EQUAL JUSTICE UNDER LAW." These words, written above the main entrance to the Supreme Court Building, express the ultimate responsibility of the Supreme Court of the United States to interpret the law.

The US Constitution does not guarantee "justice" for all. However, the US Constitution guarantees "due process" to protect a citizen from a tyrant ruler and "bear arms" for self-defense.

The old-world social wisdom "knowledge is power" is defeated by the current social structure of money, sex, drugs, democracy, and law enforcement.

Religion is the best remedy for eradicating criminality in society. But then again, religion and state have never gotten along throughout history.

For example, the King set the monotheistic religious leader Abraham (AS) on fire for treason against the government when he preached Monotheism and advised people to do good. As a result, Moses (AS) was exiled from Egypt, Jesus (AS) was crucified in Jerusalem, and Prophet Muhamed (PBUH) was expelled from

Mekkah; that is precisely the reason the founding father of the USA clearly stated, "Freedom of Religion" in the Constitution.

However, the media is obsessed with the anti-religious sentiment. For the last 70 years, the media worked relentlessly to take the entire society into publicly open sex by calling sex a taboo and strongly supporting homosexuality.

In my opinion, good parenting and a good community are the keys to a peaceful society, not the government. Lecturing 24 hours on TV talk shows about crime will not deter criminality in society. The root cause of corruption in the community is the reluctance of parents and shameless obscenity spreading in society.

The Messenger of Allah (ﷺ) said: "One of the things people have learned from the words of the earliest prophecies is, "If you do not feel any shame, do whatever you like." Related by Al-Bukhari.

These days, people do not feel a sense of respect and human dignity. A sense of respect does prevent a person from committing a petty crime. The parent's responsibility is to teach the kids human dignity, right and wrong, and not pressure them to earn money. Money is a necessity; eventually, they will understand it.

The judicial system's responsibility is to prevent evil from the community, not enforce the law in society. The law should be intended to deliver Justice rather than an excuse to make money.

In fact, knowing right and wrong in society is extinguished in the concept of all things considered.

Justice in the USA

In the USA, all politicians stated, "We are people of rules of Law," meaning they will make laws, and we all have to obey their laws; otherwise, we, the people, pay the consequences. They will decide what we, the people, can do or not.

The core principle of the Lawmaking concept in our time is the "Whim of the Clown Politicians who are lacking in common sense, knowledge, facts, and reasonings, but their mind is on vote bank and lobbyists' money." They fool the voters by luring them with false promises to win the election. Their intention is not to serve the nation with sincerity with the framework of general welfare but rather to make money and power.

To deliver "Justice," one must understand how to balance the scales of "Right and Wrong," identifying wrongdoing and the wrongdoer, which is not the legislator's thought thoroughness. Ensuring "Justice" for all is not easy because there are no guiding principles for determining right or wrong in the USA except in Islam.

Historically, in most cultures before Islam, the social structural foundation was based on muscle men's whim and desire, not on moral principles. Their understanding was that "Might is Right." Masculine, strong men controlled a tribe or nation. In other words, weak men, morally conscious men, women and girls were oppressed and humiliated by muscle men.

For example, the death sentence of Socrates was the legal consequence of asking politico-philosophic questions of his students, which resulted in the two accusations of moral corruption and impiety. At trial, the majority of the male citizen jurors chosen by lot who voted to convict him of the two charges; then, consistent with common legal practice, voted to determine his punishment and agreed to a sentence of death to be executed by Socrates's drinking a poisonous beverage of hemlock.

And the crucifixion of Jesus, who was the execution of the crucifixion of Jesus of Nazareth in the 1st century. Also, Nimrod was angry with Abraham and decided that Abraham shall be cast into the fire, and if Abraham is correct that there is a real God, then that God will save him. Abraham was cast into the fire and was saved by God. There is "No" historical evidence suggesting that any civilization had the concept of "Justice" except Islam. Every culture was built on some injustices under the strong-muscle mindset; society was significantly influenced by caste and feudal systems.

The commitment to Justice came from Islam, as the Quran stated, "O you who believe! Stand out firmly for Justice as witnesses to Allah, even though it be against yourselves, your parents, or your kin, be he rich or poor, Allah is a better Protector to both. So follow not the lusts, lest you may avoid Justice;" (4:135) and Prophet (PBUH) said: "If Fatimah bint Muhammad were to steal, I would cut off her hand."

My educated guess is that the European colonialists copied the "Justice System" from Muslims and standardized it. The tradition of colonialist Europeans put a hand on the Bible to swear in the courtroom that the victim and defendant would tell nothing but the truth.

But, nowadays, no one believes in the Bible, and no "Courtroom" has a Bible. The colonialists' concept of Lady Justice was originally Justitia, the goddess of Justice, in Roman mythology. Emperor Augustus introduced the concept of Justitia. Justice was considered a virtue, which Emperor Augustus celebrated in his clipeus virtutis, and a temple of Justitia was established in Rome by Emperor Tiberius.

In Europe, Justitia became a symbol of the virtue of Justice with which every emperor wished to associate his regime. Emperor Vespasian minted coins with the image of the goddess seated on a throne called Justitia Augusta, and many emperors after him used the idea of the goddess to proclaim themselves protectors of Justice. Justitia is an artistic symbolic personification rather than an actual goddess.

Defund The Police

There is a solid noise for defunding the police in the USA. Also, another group is raising the concern of increasing crime in megacities like NYC, LA, and San Francisco and demanding that the police remain an iron fist law enforcement department in the USA.

At the point of law and order, making laws is a constitutional duty of national, state, and local elected representatives. The Constitution does not explicitly encourage lawmakers to use their "intellectual capacity to distinguish right from wrong before making a law."

As a matter of fact, the Constitution allowed the elected representative to use their discretion when making a "law." The law can be unnecessarily wordy, ambiguous, illogical, anti-social, and anti-religious, but a police officer must enforce the law without asking a question. The police are trained to obey the orders from their superiors, and whether it is morally wrong or right must not be taken into consideration but to follow the orders.

As I witnessed, during Mayor Bloomberg's era, NYC Mayor Bloomberg orchestrated a scheme to target Muslims in NYC. I do not know whether Mayor Bloomberg strategically used Hispanic police as part of NYC administrative policy or whether Hispanic police took advantage of the NYC policy to harass Muslims.

There was a terrorist attack in Spain on March 11, 2004, that killed 193 people. I have seen most Hispanics have soft corners for Spain because Latin America was a Spanish colony, and their religious affiliation is Catholic, and so do Hispanics in the USA. Hispanics are predominantly Catholic.

However, I have seen and experienced NYPD's systematic harassment of Muslim immigrants, taxi, limo, black car, and private car drivers. When I dug into the situation, I found out most Hispanic NYPD randomly target Muslim-looking taxis, limos, black cars, and gypsy cabs to fill their summons quota and make more arrests to get promoted as detectives. The detectives receive higher salaries than regular police. Therefore, I am not fond of the police force.

There is also a social-psychological difference between Hispanic and Muslim immigrants. Most Hispanics walked into the USA illegally, crossing the land border or water, and lived or were raised in a disadvantageous social community where gang violence, drugs, rapes, prostitution, and femicide are the ongoing daily social norm. In contrast, most Muslims migrated to the USA from the middle class or upper-middle class; their social standing is far different from Hispanic. Of course, some immigrated to the USA by DV 1.2, O.P. 1, lottery programs, and student visas, and some are chain immigrants, just like myself.

NYPD found entertainment with new Muslim immigrants DV 1.2 and political asylees in the name of preventing terrorist attacks in NYC. In fact, none of the terrorist masterminds was a taxi driver until they made one to gain credibility. I have witnessed that Hispanic police were lacking in common sense and shameless liars.

NYPD's senseless, irrational behavior annihilated many Muslim families by unnecessarily pulling over and writing summons in pretext to identify the individuals that caused financial distress in the families.

I fought against NYPD and was arrested twice by the Hispanic female police. I sensed what touched their ego. To beef up their ego, dozens of summonses were written against me from 2004 to 2008 out of hateful anger and boastful arrogance to teach me a lesson.

I am fully aware of the "Do you know who I am?" egoistic disease because I was born in the upper class. Those from the lower class always tend to show off bureaucratic positions egoistically, feeling it is a power, whereas the upper class understands performing the duty ethically with honor. I paid nearly ten thousand dollars for tickets, and several times, my license was suspended due to the loss of points and unpaid fines and penalties.

The DMV judges act like robots. They make random guilty

pleas and make money. Interestingly, the police read the same note again and again. The judges do not listen to both sides' stories, as they should, to understand who lies and tells the truth. Or are they intellectually unable to comprehend that the police purposely wrote the summonses to fill the quotas, were instructed by the City Mayor to make more money for the city, or hate Muslims? It is not very easy to rationalize Judges' behaviors.

I tried to organize the Muslim Taxi Driver Association to fight against Bloomberg Muslims' discriminatory behaviors. Still, I could not because almost all Muslim Taxi, Limo, and Black Car Drivers were immigrants, and some of their asylum cases were pending. That is why they do not want to be politically organized but rather endure police harassment and pay the fine.

The history of policing in the USA is undefined. For instance, in British Colonial America, the New York Sheriff's Office was founded in 1626. the county sheriff was the most critical law enforcement official. The sheriff was elected official to enforce the law, not to do community policing.

The county sheriff, an elected official, was responsible for enforcing laws, collecting taxes, supervising elections, and handling the legal business of the county government. Sheriffs would investigate crimes and make arrests after citizens filed complaints or provided information about a crime but did not carry out patrols like nowadays. There is no substantial evidence suggesting that the sheriff's primary objective was to deter crime in the community.

Villages and cities typically hired constables and marshals, who were empowered to make arrests and serve warrants. Many municipalities also formed a night watch or group of citizen volunteers who would patrol the streets at night, looking for crime or fires.

Typically, constables and marshals were the primary law enforcement officials available during the day to look for criminal acts, while the night watch would serve during the night. Eventually, municipalities formed day watch groups. Local militias handled rioting. Once again, there is no evidence of community policing to ensure the safety of the citizens.

Policing is a new concept in the USA. What it is needs to be fully understood and well-defined. Police do multitask as ordered by their superiors. It also systematically harasses people and prey on easy targets to fill up the quota. Without them, the looters and criminals will create anarchy. And keeping them, the helpless people will be systematically abused. If people want peace in life, they have to teach the children right and wrong and reason for doing good. If there were no criminals in society, I would boldly say terminate the police department altogether. The police generate revenues for the court system and DMV at the cost of victimizing some innocent people, which creates jobs; other than that, they are used for nothing, just a burden.

In Islamic History, The Police

Messenger of Allah (ﷺ) says, "Whosoever of you sees an evil, let him change it with his hand; and if he is not able to do so, then [let him change it] with his tongue; and if he is not able to do so, then with his heart — and that is the weakest of faith." **[Muslim]**

Shurṭa is the standard Arabic term for the police. Shurṭa was established in the early days of the Caliphate, the Caliphate of Umar ibn al-Khattab (634–644). He first created Sahib-ul-Ahdath, the police chief. In the Umayyad and Abbasid Caliphates, the shurṭa had considerable responsibilities to deter criminality in the society, such as murder, rape, gambling, stealing, and fraudulent activities, and its head, the Sabib Al- Shurta was a chief official, whether at the provincial level or in the central government.

The duties of the shurṭa varied with time and place: it was primarily policing to deter haram in the society, such as murder, rape, prostitution, consumption of alcohol, and fraudulent activities and worked as an internal security force and also had judicial functions, but it could also be entrusted with enforcing the hisbah, customs, and tax duties, rubbish collection, acting as a bodyguard for governors, etc.

In the Abbasid East, the chief of police also supervised the prison system. After the 10th century, the use of the shurṭa declined, along with the authority of the Khalifate. Throughout Islamic history, Shurta's responsibility was community policing and solving minor disputes among people. Only index criminals were brought to the Qadi (judge). Only the Qadi (judge) decides the accused should be lynched, fined, imprisoned, or beheaded, whereas the British judicial system and police are much more different. In my opinion, the American justice system borrowed from the British and Islamic judicial systems.

Military Coup

A conversation begins about an expected military coup in the USA, as some politicians and media outlets deliberately push to politicize the U.S. military. It sounds like a Military Coup is appealing to many, but it may lead to a grave social consequence in the country.

They do not understand that politicizing the military organization will not be a good political strategy for the USA. The military establishment is not a political clown show, as most politicians do to get elected. But, it is an apolitical organization. They are trained armed forces to obey the "Chain of Command" command and "Respect the Chain of Command." They are under oath to defend the country from enemies. Not governing a country.

My father always said, "Ignorance is not bliss but a strategy for the corrupt politicians and tragedy for the rational society." Many people will vehemently ignore my saying and assume that "I know nothing about the military organization."

First, let me remind those people that I have received at least a dollar from the U.S. Army as a paycheck. Some of my colleagues may have become Colonel, Brigadier General, or Major General, or died in combat, or left the Army. I have not had contact with my old colleagues, friends, or co-workers for more than 20 years.

I did not feel it was necessary to keep in touch with them, and they also used to feel uncomfortable because of my outspokenness against the lie wars.

Secondly, my blood relatives are cultural nephews and in English culture, the second cousin in the 1971 India-Pakistan war was the Bangladesh War General. Thirdly, in the 1971 Indian-Pakistan war, my father was the "Peace Committee Standing Committee Chairman." In East Pakistan, all the Pro-Pakistani guerrilla Razakers, Al-Badr, Al-Shams, and Islamic Mujahedeen were under my father's leadership.

Therefore, I do not need any lectures from whimsical opinionists to educate me on how a chain of command works. Since I was a baby, I have heard all the military strategies. I have a wealth of knowledge about conventional war and guerrilla war. The military is disciplined into one understanding, the "Chain of command." If the junior officers do not respect the high command, the eventual outcome is a military coup d'état that may lead to random civilian casualties.

However, historically, the military has two segments: Officers and Enlisted. In the Old World, officers were recruited from noble families and fought for their family honors. The enlisted were recruited from pagans, peasants, slaves, and many other lower-class or low-income people by alluring their bread and butter.

Throughout history, all coups were committed by officers who were well-connected with each other through bloodlines or marriages.

To the point, a coup appeals to some people because they believe "Might is Right." They believe the military will discipline the nation. A military takeover means suspending the "constitution" and imposing "martial law." This means that citizens will not be able to enjoy their constitutional rights.

Suppose you are highly punctual in your duties. Yes. "Martial Law" is a good thing; otherwise, it is a nightmare for most people. But, the USA has fifty states, and some states will refuse to accept the autocracy. In other words, civil war or breaking of the Union. The bottom line is that breaking the "Chain of Command" could end the USA.

Sex Politics

"Sex" is a hot topic in the USA. Every day, news media talk about it on the T.V. channels and have some "Breaking News" on it. Sex is a natural, healthy part of all living things that should be fun and pleasurable.

But then again, thousands of years ago, religion restricted human sex. Religion considers sex outside of marriage as a sin. Also, the marriage was intended for the general welfare of the child and their family identity. However, sex has never been a political issue throughout history. It is more like a religious issue. On the contrary, in the USA, the media makes sex a central domestic and international political issue.

As a former student of Criminal Justice at Mercy College from 1997-2001, and have done an internship in 2000 at the Bronx Criminal Court with the CJA. I am well-informed about sex in the USA.

My study showed that the sexual revolution occurred in the USA during the 60s with the porn movie known as the sexual revolution, which created high volumes of domestic violence in the country and the 80s homosexuality revolution.

However, homosexuality is not a new sexual activity in society. It has existed throughout history and the World. In our class participation, sex was highly discussed and debated because of the Bill Clinton sex scandal.

In my opinion, the sex war is in the USA in its suicide mission that creates a toxic social discord. As old people used to say, "Women's jealousy does not have wisdom." Traditional wisdom related to women is that "Women's jealousy can burn a house without remorse." We can see that women disregard family values and seek divorce more than men. To women, financial security is more important than family values.

Historically, women were sold as a sexual commodity for the strip club, prostitution, and for the king's court to entertain lords, knights, and foreign diplomats. Only the noble class and lords' families hid their girls and women inside the house in the name of family honor.

If a woman or a girl violated traditional family honor, they used to kill them in the name of family honor or bury them alive. Quran put this question to men: "When the female infant (Al-Maw'udah) buried alive is questioned (Su'ilat):. For what sin was she killed" Al-Quran (81:8-9).

The monotheistic religious leader Prophet Abraham (AS) advocated that people should marry women for virtue, decency, and modesty and build a happy family, not only for sex. As the Quran mentioned, "And among His signs is this that He created for you wives from among yourselves, that you may find repose in them, and He has put between you affection and mercy. Verily, in that, are indeed signs for a people who reflect" Al-Quran (30:21). But then again, Al-Quran emphasizes "affection and mercy," not sex.

Islam changed the perception of women from sexual commodities to wives and mothers. Jahimah came to the Prophet (ﷺ) and said: "O Messenger of Allah! I want to go out and fight (in Jihad), and I have come to ask your advice." He said: "Do you have a mother?" He said: "Yes." He said: "Then stay with her, for Paradise is beneath her feet." Sunan an-Nasa'i (3104).

In thousands of years of governmental history, sex politics was never part of the state's politics. The "so-called judicial system used handled only the rape cases." Of course, the judicial system was not impartial. The judges always took the side of the traders, landlords, or the King's court officials.

However, during the Industrial Revolution, women faced high physical and verbal abuse rates in the USA and Europe. Men worked 12-18 hours a day, 6-7 days a week, which led to, on April 21st, 1856, part of the eight-hour workday movement. And alcohol consumption was skyrocketing. That is why a nationwide constitutional ban on the production, importation, transportation, and sale of alcoholic beverages from 1920 to 1933 was imposed on production, importation, and sale in the USA. Alcohol consumption was one of the primary reasons for increasing domestic violence. Secondly, long manual labor working hours.

Why do long manual labor hours cause domestic violence? The study showed that manual working makes the man sexually active. When a man goes home after long hours of work, he takes a shower and eats dinner. After that, he wants sex, but women mostly say no to sex, which angers the man, and he beats her up and frequently accuses her of having an affair with another man. In a few cases, the man was right. Some women used to have affairs with good-looking and wealthy guys.

Constitutionally, women were allowed to freely assemble to organize themselves to fight for their voting rights. During the Industrial Revolution, as domestic violence increased throughout the USA, women organized themselves to pressure politicians to give women the right to vote. The 19th Amendment to the U.S. Constitution, which granted American women the right to vote, was passed by Congress on June 4th, 1919, and ratified on August 18th, 1920.

In recent days, the media obsession with sex has made it a sex politics in the USA. On the other hand, corrupt politicians are hungry for media attention to become famous and vote bank; that is why they promote media bias on the political stage without moral consciousness and understanding of the social issues. That annihilated the family-oriented social structure in the USA.

Historically, sexual behavior was restricted by the monotheistic religious leader Prophet Abraham (AS) in the name of virtue, decency, and modesty. Besides religion, the noble class limited their girls to free mixing with their male counterparts, fearing falling in love with the commoners or getting impregnated without traditional family ceremonies and dishonoring the family values. If any girls violate the traditional family nobility, they kill them or bury them alive. Some of the commoners learned the family honors by observing the noble class; that is why it is called common law marriage.

Generally, common law marriage was religiously considered fornication. However, the noble class used to call it commoners' marriage for their political agenda. Throughout history, authority and religion have never gotten along. Only Islamic Khalifat took complete control of religion and politics. After that, only one country in the New World wrote in the constitution "freedom of religion."

However, in the New World, Churches lost their credibility in religious teaching. Now, it is only symbolic entertainment. The point is crystal clear that sex was and is restricted by religion; the State has nothing to do with it. The authorities never cared for sex;

instead, they created a designated area for the sex business known as prostitution, brothel or the Red District. The lowest of the traditional social classes, such as the pagans, pageants, slaves, Dalits, serfs, and shudra., used to do their marriage ceremony if they affiliated with any religion; otherwise, they had sex with whomever they wanted without any restriction.

In our times, most politicians come from the bottom; that is why they do not understand the concept of prestige. It is okay for them to have sex with whomever they want, but they love to legislate sex. The average sexual partner is 7 in the USA.

Why is the media making it a clown show, and lawmakers keep making sex laws? The media tells us that Politicians are a new moral authority, whereas most politicians are morally bankrupt.

Women Rights

*"Messenger of Allah (PBUH) said, "The most perfect man in his faith among the believers is the one whose behavior is most excellent, and the best of you are those who are the best to their wives." **(At- Tirmidhi)***

USA media obsession with propagating "Women's Rights." Women are the majority in the USA. The US media capitalized on women's rights and tried to create a political Olympic game worldwide that upset many world heads of state.

The US media misunderstands the world leader's tolerance of USA media. The reason most "Heads of State" tolerate the USA is that most foreign countries use the Dollar as their trade currency. In 1977, the USA passed a law to sanction foreign countries that are not the USA's lovely boys. In other words, they fear the freezing of assets.

Women's rights are not crystal clear, as I have spoken with hundreds of women to understand the rights they are looking for and from whom they want their rights. Not one single woman was able to answer my question with satisfaction.

Some women want a right man; some want a real man; some want to have sex with whomever they wish to like a man; some do not want kids; they want abortion rights, and some want equal pay from their employers.

In my understanding, they were brainwashed by the media that women receive less than men from their employers; therefore, they need a right.

As we know, the gender wage gap has been a political issue in the U.S. since 1860. Women's rights activists Susan B. Anthony and Elizabeth Cady Stanton were among the movement's most vigorous advocates, making a case for equal pay in their newspaper, The Revolution, and other works. It was not until the ratification of the 19th Amendment to the Constitution in 1920 that women won the right to vote in the U.S. However, it was not until the 1940s that a bill was introduced to prohibit discrimination in pay on account of sex. Unfortunately, the bill never made it through Congress.

The 1960s saw significant steps for equal pay and civil rights in the United States. The Equal Pay Act of 1963 prohibited employers from paying male and female workers different wages for jobs that required equal skill, effort, and responsibility. However, exceptions were allowed, such as pay structures based on seniority or merit.

President John F. Kennedy called paying men and women different wages for the same work an "unconscionable practice," citing the statistic that "the average woman worker earns only 60%

of the average wage for men." A year later, Title VII of the Civil Rights Act of 1964 broadened the law to make compensation decisions based on race, color, religion, sex, or national origin unlawful, with similar exceptions.

In the 1970s and 1980s, the concept of comparable worth, also known as pay equity, entered the national conversation. Proponents of comparable worth called attention to wage gaps among workers in jobs that, while not identical, could be considered similar in terms of skills, responsibility, and value to the overall enterprise. Often, those gaps were a legacy of past discrimination. While comparable worth made little progress on the federal level, it did become law in several states.

"Women's Rights" is an ambiguous human expression without a logical solution. However, Islam never said to pay less because they are women.

In other words, women need to make their own decisions. What do they like to be? The solution to their problem is the self-realization of their own body and the nature of the men. Women's body is complex than men's. In Islam, there are two looks: internal and external. We all look externally; most problems can be solved if we start looking internally. Law-making is not a solution for human sexual behavior that is human nature. It cannot be legislated. It needs to train self-control by fearing God's Punishment on the Day of Judgment. The law is meant to deter and prevent anti-social elements.

Racial Politics

*"O mankind! We have created you from a male and a female and made you into nations and tribes where you may know one another. Verily, the most honorable of you with Allah is that (believer) who has At-Taqwa. Verily, Allah is All-Knowing, All-Aware." **Al-Quran 49:13***

In a racially divided USA, Black and White is a highly politicized topic. More commonly discussed in the media, the root cause of racism in the USA is the slavery history in the USA. In the eighteenth century, black people in the USA were brought as slaves against their will from the African continent. Historically, the slave trade was an ancient trade throughout the World. It was not invented in the USA.

The landowners only bought slaves to do plantation and housemaids. Not all the so-called "Whites" were slave owners. Some of the "White" people could not even feed themselves one time in a day.

I do not understand why the entire "White" population has to bear the burden of master and slaves' guilt. That is a good question.

On the other hand, some landowners treated black women like queens because they gave birth to many babies. Some

Landlords dehumanized some lazy black people by lynching, murdering, and raping. The question is whether Black people are a dilemma or a blessing for the USA.

The US Media is imposing on the minds of "White" people that "Whites" are superior to black people and that whites enjoy white privilege. In fact, some landlords during industrialization avoided official contact with the slaves by hiring fair-skinned people who created racism. The landowners were the leading investors of most companies; that is why companies' management used to respect their wishes. That is how racial discrimination was taught in the workplace, and it spread throughout the nation.

During industrialization, fair-skinned people were not treated as well as some assumed; they worked 12-18 hours a day, which led to 8 working 8-hour movement. The only difference was labeling the working class and blacks were slaves.

In most cases, slaves were better off. Their masters provided their basic needs, such as shelter, food, clothes, etc., while the working class had to provide everything independently.

Recently, a North Korean defector student studied at an Ivy League university. According to her statement, "The IVY League Universities" systematically brainwash students to hate "white people," which was published on June 14, 2021. By hating "White" people, some opportunist built their careers in media and politics.

In the ancient world, people used to identify themselves with their tribes and the emperor like Al-Hindi, Misri, Cina, Roman, Persian, etc.

For example, in Islamic history, Arabs say, "Arabs are white, Romanians (Europeans) are red, and Africans are black, etc. Islam eradicates slavery by buying them to free them for sin forgiveness. The Prophet (ﷺ) ordered us to free slaves at the time of solar eclipses. Sahih al-Bukhari 2519.

In the USA, the fair-skinned people fought against slavery to liberate them in 1861. I think it is time for fair-skinned people to realize that skin color does not make any of us superior. Skin color is an ancient politics to keep the group strong. Logically, different kinds of skinned people make people feel like strangers to each other and question their reliability.

We need to understand that criminals, fraud, prostitutes, con artists, cheaters, rapists, and disloyal people do not belong to only one skin color of people. We can find them in every race or color of skin.

Black and White is a social issue, not a political issue. The challenge is that they hate each other based on skin color. It is not a legal matter. The so-called "Law" can only be in the law library as a means to make money, but it will not resolve this issue.

If all Americans, "White," realized that only the landowners had slaves for the plantation that day, the issue of blacks and whites would ease the racial tension.

Otherwise, the country will remain divided on the racial line. The "whites" also need to understand that they were also slaves under Rome and Muslims. Every one of us needs to stop unnecessarily hating each other based on race. It is time to come to the senses and eliminate all the nonsense.

Voter Fraud

The concept of voter fraud exists throughout the world. The US media vehemently defends that there was no voter fraud in the 2020 election.

What is the voter fraud? Electoral fraud, also known as election manipulation, voter fraud, or vote rigging, is a severe issue that affects the integrity of voting processes worldwide. This illegal interference can take many forms, such as increasing the vote share of a favored candidate or depressing the vote share of rival candidates. Unfortunately, voter suppression often goes hand-in-hand with electoral fraud. While the definition of electoral fraud varies from country to country, the ultimate goal is often the same: to subvert the democratic process. The Election Commission must remain vigilant in identifying and combatting electoral fraud to ensure free and fair elections.

I have been very familiar with the word voter fraud throughout my life. My dad ran for the United Pakistan National Assembly in Pakistan on December 7, 1970. In the election, he was defeated by one of my blood relatives, MAG Osmani, by a landslide. My dad always maintained that that election was 100% fraudulent.

Even though MAG Osmani was his relative, I went to Osmani's house with my dad a few times. If I remember correctly, my dad always raised this issue in their private conversation. Osmani had technically admitted to my dad that the election was fraudulent. Osmani did say, "I was in India for eight months as a War General. I did witness Indian Intelligence Direct Interference in our matters".

I was also a victim of voter fraud in NYC. In 1997, I was running for Mercy College Student president on the Mercy College Manhattan Campus. My opponent, the presidential candidate, openly wrote the student's name and signed the name sheet. He put all the ballots in the Ballot Box. I also witnessed voter fraud in the 2008 Election in Jamaica, Queens.

Commonly understood, voter fraud involves a person or election officials casting a vote for a person who has never cast their ballot. A registered voter might not be casting a vote, have moved out of the voter registration address, or be dead. However, the voter list was not correctly updated prior to Election Day.

Voter fraud is a political cancer throughout the world that will remain in the election process forever. There is no cure for it.

Some of the power-hunger will deliberately defraud the system. Or a blind supporter will intentionally try to trick the electoral system into favoring their favorite candidate.

2020 Election Drama

I was expecting the US 2020 election would turn out to be a dramatic political theater, and the media would create thunderstorm news coverage against Trump with dehumanization and humiliation content. My thought had proven meticulously correct.

The reason I feel that the 2020 election would be dramatic political theater. Actually, in 2015, I left home to go to Dallas. At LaGuardia Airport, I bought a newspaper to read on the plane. That newspaper was the New York Times. During the flight airtime, I read an interesting analytical article to pass my time.

The article heavily concentrates on Mr. Trump's characteristically indecent behavior, which hints that Mr. Trump is a womanizer. I started laughing on the plane. A few passengers were staring at me strangely. The next seated passenger asked me, "Where I am from?" I smiled at him and said, "Sylhet, Bangladesh." He said, "You speak good English." I said, "I have no choice. I am 3rd generation chain immigrant, and English is my first language. He said, "Oh, I am sorry. I meant, are you from New York or Dallas?" I said, "Jamaica, Queens." He said, "That is why you are attentively reading this article." I said, "You are profiling, but you are correct." As a matter of fact, Mr. Trump was from Jamaica. Jamaica Muslim Center is very close to Wexford.

What made me laugh, in my mind, was saying that the way the article attempted character assassination on Mr. Trump would not work in the USA for the reason that the average number of sexual partners for men and women in the United States is 7. It may work in Saudi Arabia but not in the USA. The writers attempted a character assassination, which is nothing but stupidity.

Since 2015, I have written every day on Mr. Trump's Official Facebook page until 2019, when I deleted my FaceBook page. All of my predictions turned out to be true and accurate, except ousting him from the Presidency.

I have predicted that Mr. Trump has a high possibility of winning the 2016 election. If he wins, he will face strong resistance from the media outlets, including calls for impeaching him and eventually trying to oust him from the Presidency.

Rigged Election

As I was expecting the 2020 election to be rigged, history teaches us a lesson. My paternal grandfather was a founding member of the Muslim League. The main objective of the Muslim League was to liberate Muslims from Hindu Upper caste and British slavery (Proza). To solve the problem of slavery (Proza), the Muslim League decided to create a Muslim country. Abul Kalam Azad, a Congress leader, warned the Muslim League that "it would not last more than 25 years if they made Pakistan".

Yes. Pakistan was dismembered within 25 years. Original Pakistan became Bangladesh, and West Pakistan became Pakistan.

How did that happen? Very simple. Brainwashing technique. 98% of East Bengali were Hindu Proza. They did not know how to read or write. The Indian Intelligence (I.B.) used the Hindu minority to brainwash East Pakistani Bengali into Bengali Nationalism to dismember the United Pakistan. There was only one objective by all means necessary to prevent Pakistani integration by demonizing Pakistanis and separating East Pakistanis as Bengalis.

The Hindu minority was highly educated at the time of partition in 1947. They dominated the East Pakistan bureaucracy and public educational institutions such as primary schools, high schools, colleges, and universities. Similar brainwashing mechanisms U.S. media and establishment created to dehumanize only Trump. The critical role played by most Ivy League university graduates, most Ivy League-educated bureaucrats, they structurally created a bureaucratic elite class commonly known to Trump supporters as the "Deep State."

The brainwashing mechanisms focused on public high schools, Community Colleges and Universities to gain the majority of the women's anger.

They deliberately intended to create fear in Homosexual

and Hispanic communities. As a matter of fact, the USA is not culturally a religious country where Homosexuality is the slightest concern.

They also try to capitalize on the "Muslim Ban" to gain Muslim support. In contrast, Muslims are an insignificant minority who were systematically victimized over decades in the name of preventing terrorists attack, and it is hard to scare them because they believe in Qadr. However, I consistently write on Trump's official Facebook page and encourage Muslims to vote for Trump.

And then again, every action reacts; Mr. Trump's supporters were brainwashed into "white superiority" for a long time. Ms. Hillary Clinton referred to them as a "Basket of deplorable," and they were angry at President Barack Hussein Obama's Presidency.

In reality, Barack Hussein Obama was not lineal with American slaves, who had a complex identity. He was the son of a free African man who came to the USA to study, and his mother was a free Caucasian woman. They did not understand that chemistry. They looked at him as a Muslim, black, and inferior class.

Even though the Constitution is crystal clear on "Freedom of Religion," it does not matter whether Barack Hussein Obama is a Muslim or Christian. The Constitution gave the full right to be one. But the media brainwashed the nation with the idea that Muslim means terrorist and un-American and Black are of slave descent.

The Media portrays Mr. Trump as a real danger to women and minorities. According to the Census Bureau, the majority of the population is women in the USA. The traditional and religious-affiliated women always prefer a man's leadership over a woman's. They do not have confidence in women's leadership. But the feminists were hardcore supporters of Ms. Hillary Clinton. Ms. Clinton called them "deplorable," which backfired; these are some of the factors that made Mr. Trump win the 2016 election, which media and establishment could not digest.

The minority is a combination of legal and illegal various ethnicity, social status, religious affiliation, and political backgrounds. Those whose parents came illegally to the USA, parents had very adventurous and deceiving countries that immigration authorities experienced, which stories narrated to their children. They are good at being street-smart. Their parents cross the borders illegally, which means they have fooled many law-enforcement agents to enter the USA. In their childhood memory, they have heard all the tricks and techniques to deceive from parents.

Practically speaking, if the underage can get into the bar to buy and drink alcohol with a fake I.D., why can't they vote for people who do not live at the same address on Election Day? A hundred street smarts can easily cast more than a thousand votes. Logically, eleven million undocumented immigrant children in the USA can do funny things to defeat Mr. Trump in the 2020 election.

I have frequently requested Mr. Trump to concede the election. Otherwise, the situation will get much more complicated. He cannot legally prove the election was rigged because once the vote is cast, it is impossible to prove the illegality of the counted vote. It is challenging to identify the voter. The legal theory requires substantial evidence, which is impossible to demonstrate in a case like this.

My prediction has proven correct again. On January 6th, 2021, some hot-tempered, ignorant people flooded into Capitol Hill.

What next. It was impossible to reverse the election outcome in the world. Throughout election history, there is no evidence of reversing the election result. According to the election theory, vote cast, recount the ballot or declare re-election if a dispute arises. The election result may lead a nation to civil war or civil violence.

No 1, the recount does not make any significant difference. Fraudulent voters are good street smart. They know how to defraud the system.

No.2, re-election that will not happen in USA. In USA history, the re-election never occurred because the electorates elect the president, not the popular vote. The idea of re-election will touch the ego of the states. They will feel the insult to their credibility and will refuse re-election.

No.3, a civil war. For example, the 1970 election in Pakistan. The election result led to a civil war in 1971 and dismembered United Pakistan forever. However, a civil war is beyond imagination in the USA because the US election in the USA is not based on ideology, and both parties do not have a fine line on doctrine. They do not have well-trained ideological cadres to be aggressive with much animation. Therefore, a civil war in the USA is beyond imagination.

2020 Election

I am writing this piece based on the argument established in the media that Trump lost the election and he must concede. Most media jokers are intellectually incapacitated to comprehend the US political process, the reason behind the election, and its merit.

Their thoughtless talk clearly indicates that this country is in real danger because these talk shows feed millions of citizens their ignorance. Those citizens will engage in coffee tables, living rooms, and bar conversations, leading to ignorance.

The 2020 election was filled with drama, unpredictability, and talk show criticism of President Trump vehemently; the media expected Mr. Joe Bidden to be the United States of America president, which led to media outrage against Mr. Trump, and the election has become a clown show instead of choosing a moral characteristic Head of the Union.

In the USA, media interference in the political process created a movie-like situation rather than a severe political determination against rightful nation leaders.

The "Freedom of the Press" is a fundamental Constitutional right. It does not necessarily mean that the media is the president, politicians, senators, governors, and policymakers.

Let me share with the readers the historical reason behind the election. In the early 16th century, some English men debated in secret about holding an election to engage the noble class in the political decision-making process in the Kingdom. The King used to make a whimsical decision that created social and religious discord in England and caused constant social unrest.

As history witnessed, the King was an absolute monarchy governing system throughout the World except for the Islamic Khalifate. King Henry the Eighth declared himself Head of the Church and had two of his wives executed, which angered the Church and The Lords.

Trump, The Warrior

On August 22nd, 1642, the English Civil War broke out. The Parliamentarian won the civil war. At the same time, the British government was weakened which led to the East India Company becoming more administratively and politically powerful until Queen Victoria took decisive action against the East India Company in 1857 to dismantle the company altogether.

According to the US Constitution, the USA is a selectively elected representative "Republic," not a popularly democratically elected "Centralized Presidency." Secondly, The Federal President or Union President is elected by the Electoral College, not by the "popular vote." The Electoral College has the constitutional duty to make sure the President is qualified to be the US president or not. The Electoral College does the vetting process by verifying his Citizenship, moral character, patriotism, leadership skills, etc. The Electoral College has the constitutional right to overturn the popular vote if necessary.

Most Americans are not well educated in the political and governmental system in the USA, which may cause substantial problems in the country shortly. Americans, even some Ph.D. holders, need a basic understanding of the US system. They may believe any foolishness that may cause worse upheaval than January 6th.

A brain-dead said on the talk show that Trump voters'

children and grandchildren would regret voting for Trump. Individually, in the USA, the average number of sexual partners is 7. To find out a birth father requires a DNA test. As of today, this is the reality of the social structure of the USA. It seemed to me that the brain-dead did not know the new US social structure is individualism. Not a family-oriented society. My question is, where will the grandchildren or great-grandchildren come from?

By the way, after all the vicious media dehumanization, he received more than 70 million votes in person; that being said, his supporters did like him. If there had been no doubtful mail-in vote, vote harvesting, computer glitch, or clerical error, he would have been the Media's projected winner.

Trump's incitement of hate

The US media and their commentator always accuse Trump of incitement of hate. The hate and violence have been on the rise in the USA for decades, and it is not all about Trump. Muslims have been particularly affected by hateful rhetoric, which is having a profound impact on how their neighbors and schoolmates treat them. Unfortunately, this toxic rhetoric has become part of U.S. mainstream discourse, with dangerous consequences. It is time for all of us to take individual responsibility for the words we use and the impact they have. Not scapegoating Trump. We must work together to create a more respectful and accepting society where hate has no place.

95

The January 6th

On January 6, 2021, the United States Capitol Building in Washington, D.C., was attacked by a mob of supporters of then-U.S. president Donald Trump, two months after his defeat in the 2020 presidential election. They sought to keep Trump in power by occupying the Capitol and preventing a joint session of Congress from counting the Electoral College votes to formalize the victory of President-elect Joe Biden. The attack was ultimately unsuccessful in stopping the certification of the election results.

Within 36 hours, five people died: one was shot by Capitol Police, another died of a drug overdose, and three died of natural causes, including a police officer. Many people were injured, including 174 police officers. Four officers who responded to the attack died by suicide within seven months.

Democrats accused the January 6 incident was encouraged by Trump. On January 5 and 6, thousands of his supporters gathered in Washington, D.C., to support his claims that the 2020 election had been "stolen by emboldened radical-left Democrats" and to demand that then-Vice President Mike Pence and Congress reject Biden's victory. Starting at noon on January 6, at a "Save America" rally on the Ellipse, Trump gave a speech in which he repeated claims of election irregularities and said, "If you do not fight like hell, you are not going to have a country anymore." As

Congress began the electoral vote count, thousands of attendees walked to the Capitol, with hundreds breaching police perimeters. Among the supporters were leaders of the Proud Boys and the Oath Keepers groups, who assumably conspired to use violence and interfere with the procedural transfer of power.

More than 2,000 Trump supporters entered the building, with many accused of vandalizing and looting, including the offices of then-House Speaker Nancy Pelosi and other Congress members. Trump's supporters were also accused of assaulting Capitol Police officers and reporters and attempting to capture and harm lawmakers. A gallows was erected west of the Capitol, with supporters chanting "Hang Mike Pence" after he rejected requests from Trump and others to use his authority to overturn the Electoral College votes.

On January 6, 2021, the United States Capitol experienced a historically new upheaval by the Trump supporters that never experienced before. According to various News media reports, the breach resulted in the evacuation and lockdown of both chambers of Congress and several buildings in the Complex. Pipe bombs and Molotov cocktails were discovered, and rioters occupied the empty Senate Chamber while federal law enforcement officers defended the evacuated House floor.

Despite the gravity of the situation, President Trump

initially resisted sending the National Guard to quell the mob and later reasserted the claim that the election was "fraudulent" in a Twitter video. The Capitol was cleared of supporters by mid-evening, and the electoral vote count was resumed and completed by the early morning of January 7.

A week after the attack, the House of Representatives impeached Trump for incitement of insurrection, making him the only U.S. president to be impeached twice. In February, the Senate voted in favor of conviction but fell short of the required two-thirds, resulting in his acquittal. Senate Republicans blocked a bill to create a bipartisan, independent commission to investigate the attack, so the House instead approved a select investigation committee consisting of seven Democrats and two Republicans.

More than 1,200 people have been charged with federal crimes relating to the attack, with numerous plotters convicted of seditious conspiracy. As of December 2023, over 700 defendants had pleaded guilty or been convicted at trial, with the longest sentence given to then-Proud Boy chairman Enrique Tarrio, who was sentenced to 22 years in prison. The upheaval in the Capitol was shocking for many and an unprecedented event in American history.

Domestic reactions

In the aftermath of the attack, after drawing widespread

condemnation from the U.S. Congress, members of his administration, and the media, 45th U.S. President Donald Trump released a videotaped statement on January 7 to stop the resignations of his staff and the threats of impeachment or removal from office. In the statement, he condemned the violence at the U.S. Capitol, saying that "a new administration will be inaugurated," which was widely seen as a concession, and his "focus now turns to ensure a smooth, orderly, and seamless transition of power" to the Joe Biden administration. Vanity Fair reported that Trump was at least partially convinced to make the statement by U.S. Senator Lindsey Graham (R-SC), who told Trump a sufficient number of Senate Republicans would support removing him from office unless he conceded. Kayleigh McEnany, the White House Press Secretary, had attempted to distance the administration from the supporters' behavior in a televised statement earlier in the day. On January 9, The New York Times reported that Trump had told White House aides he regretted committing to an orderly transition of power and would never resign from office. In a March 25 interview on Fox News, Trump defended the Capitol attackers, saying they were patriots who posed "zero threat," and he criticized law enforcement for "persecuting" them.

The Joint Chiefs of Staff stated on January 12 condemning the attack and reminding military personnel everywhere that incoming President Joe Biden was about to become their commander-in-chief, saying, "... the rights of freedom of speech and assembly do not give anyone the right to resort to violence, sedition, and insurrection". The statement also said, "As we have done throughout our history, the U.S. military will obey lawful orders from the civilian leadership, support civilian authorities to protect lives and property, ensure public safety in accordance with the law, and remain fully committed to protecting and defending the Constitution of the United States against all enemies, foreign and domestic." U.S. Senator Mitch McConnell (R–K.Y.), then the Senate Majority Leader, called it a "failed insurrection," that "the mob was fed lies," and "the president and other powerful people provoked them." Christopher Wray, the director of the Federal Bureau of Investigation (FBI) since 2017, later characterized the incident as domestic terrorism. President Biden, who described the upheaval as "terrorists" aimed at "overturning the will of the American people" later shared this opinion. In early 2021, the RAND Corporation released a framework to reduce the risk of extremist activity in the U.S. military.

House Speaker Nancy Pelosi lowered the flags at the Capitol to half-staff in honor of Brian Sicknick, a United States Capitol Police officer who died following the attacks. While President Biden, Vice President Pence, and Pelosi offered condolences to Sicknick's family, former President Trump did not.

In the aftermath of Sicknick's death, Senator Ted Cruz faced criticism for previous speeches perceived as calls for violence.

A new survey by the Hobby School of Public Affairs at the University of Houston revealed that nearly a third of Texas Republicans supported the attack on the Capitol. At the same time, 83% of all Texans who expressed an opinion were opposed to it. Meanwhile, a poll of Americans just after the attack showed that 79% of those surveyed believed America was "falling apart." In February 2022, the Republican National Committee referred to the events of January 6 as "legitimate political discourse."

Joe Biden, Kamala Harris, civil rights groups, and celebrities criticized the Capitol Police for a perceived "double standard" in the treatment of the mostly "white protesters." Michelle Obama wrote, "Yesterday made it painfully clear that certain Americans are, in fact, allowed to denigrate the flag and symbols of our nation. They have just got to look the right way." Capitol Police Chief Steven Sund, who later resigned, explained they had prepared for a peaceful protest but were overwhelmed by an "angry, violent mob."

2024 presidential eligibility of Donald Trump

There are a few people who raise the question of Trump running for the 2024 Election. They tried to legally disqualify him from running for the 2024. However, their legal battle failed to prevent him from running.

Donald Trump's eligibility to run in the 2024 U.S. presidential election was the subject of a legal challenge due to his involvement in the January 6 upheaval through the 14th Amendment to the U.S. Constitution's "insurrection clause," which disqualifies insurrectionists against the United States from holding office if they have previously taken an oath to support the Constitution. Courts or officials in three states—Colorado, Maine, and Illinois—ruled that Trump was barred from presidential ballots. However, the Supreme Court in Trump v. Anderson (2024) reversed the ruling in Colorado on the basis that states could not enforce the insurrection clause against federal elected officials.

In December 2023, the Colorado Supreme Court in Anderson v. Griswold ruled that Trump had engaged in insurrection and was ineligible to hold the office of President and ordered that he be removed from the state's primary election ballots as a result. Later that same month, Maine Secretary of State Shenna Bellows also ruled that Trump engaged in insurrection and was, therefore, ineligible to be on the state's primary election ballot. An Illinois judge ruled Trump was ineligible for ballot access in the state in February 2024. All three states had their decisions unanimously reversed by the United States Supreme Court.

Previously, the Minnesota Supreme Court and the Michigan Court of Appeals both ruled that their state courts cannot apply presidential eligibility to primary elections but did not rule on the issues for a general election. By January 2024, formal challenges to Trump's eligibility had been filed in at least 34 states.

On January 5, 2024, the Supreme Court granted a writ of certiorari for Trump's appeal of the Colorado Supreme Court ruling in Anderson v. Griswold and heard oral arguments on February 8. On March 4, 2024, the Supreme Court issued a verdict unanimously reversing the Colorado Supreme Court decision, ruling that states had no authority to remove Trump from their ballots.

Anti-Trump have also argued for disqualification because of democratic backsliding and the paradox of tolerance. They say that voters should not be able to elect Donald Trump, whom they see as a threat to the Democracy.

Historic Significance

In the aftermath of the American Civil War, the 14th Amendment was enacted. Section 3 of the Amendment prohibits anyone from holding public office if they had previously engaged in insurrection or rebellion against the United States or given aid to its enemies.

Opponents of former President Trump cite his role in the January 6 United States Capitol protests as a reason for his disqualification from seeking public office. Under Section 3, a state may also determine that Trump is disqualified from appearing on its ballot.

While Trump could appeal any disqualification in court, a court action could also be brought against him seeking his disqualification under Section 3. The 14th Amendment itself provides a path for Congress to allow such a candidate to run, but this would require a vote of two-thirds of each House to remove the disqualification.

Impeachments

Impeachment is a constitutional process by which a legislative body or other legally constituted tribunal initiates charges against a public official for misconduct. It may be understood as a unique process involving both political and legal elements. In the United States, impeachment is the first of two stages; a majority vote of the House may impeach an official, but conviction and removal from office in the Senate require "the concurrence of two-thirds of the members present."

The U.S. House of Representatives has impeached an official 21 times since 1789: four times for presidents, 15 times for federal judges, once for a Cabinet secretary, and once for a senator.

Of the 21, the Senate voted to remove 8 (all federal judges) from office. The four impeachments of presidents were: Andrew Johnson in 1868, Bill Clinton in 1998, and Donald Trump in 2019 and again in 2021. All four impeachments were followed by acquittal in the Senate.

Impeachment is a constitutional remedy for severe offenses against the system of government. Its purpose is not punishment; instead, its function is primarily to maintain constitutional government. According to the House practice manual, "It is the first step in a remedial process—that of removal from public office and possible disqualification from holding further office."

While the Constitution states that "Judgment in Cases of Impeachment shall not extend further than to removal from Office, and disqualification to hold and enjoy any Office of honor, Trust or Profit under the United States," it is generally accepted that "a former President may be prosecuted for crimes of which the Senate acquitted him." In fact, an impeachment process was also commenced against Richard Nixon, but he resigned in 1974 to avoid an impeachment vote.

In Principle, impeachment is a crucial aspect of the United States governing system, as it serves as a constitutional remedy to address severe offenses against the corrupt governmental elected and appointed officials and maintain trustworthiness to the public.

President Donald Trump Impeached

The first impeachment of President Donald Trump occurred on December 18, 2019. On that date, the House of Representatives adopted two articles of impeachment against Trump: abuse of power and obstruction of Congress. On February 5, 2020, the Senate voted to acquit Trump on both articles of impeachment.

Trump's first impeachment took place after a formal House inquiry found that he had solicited foreign interference in the 2020 U.S. presidential election to help his re-election bid and had then obstructed the investigation itself by telling his administration officials to ignore subpoenas for documents and testimony. The inquiry reported that Trump withheld military aid[a] and an invitation to the White House from Ukrainian president Volodymyr Zelenskyy in order to influence Ukraine to announce an investigation into Trump's political opponent, Joe Biden, and to promote a discredited conspiracy theory that Ukraine, not Russia, was behind interference in the 2016 presidential election. The inquiry stage of Trump's impeachment lasted from September to November 2019 in the wake of an August whistleblower complaint alleging Trump's abuse of power. In October, three congressional committees deposed witnesses. In November, the House Intelligence Committee held a number of hearings at which witnesses testified publicly; on

December 3, the committee voted 13–9 (along party lines) to adopt a final report. A set of impeachment hearings before the House Judiciary Committee began on December 4; on December 13, the committee voted 23–17 (along party lines) to recommend articles of impeachment for abuse of power and obstruction of Congress. Two days later, the full House approved both articles in a mostly party-line vote. Trump is the third U.S. president in history to be impeached and the first to be impeached without support for the impeachment from his party.

The articles of impeachment were submitted to the Senate on January 16, 2020, initiating an impeachment trial. The trial saw no witnesses or documents being subpoenaed, as Republican senators rejected attempts to introduce subpoenas. On February 5, Trump was acquitted on both counts by the Senate, as neither count received 67 votes to convict. In Article I, abuse of power, the vote was 48 for conviction and 52 for acquittal. On Article II, obstruction of Congress, the vote was 47 for conviction and 53 for acquittal. Republican Mitt Romney, the only senator to break party lines, became the first U.S. senator to vote to convict a president of his party in an impeachment trial, voting to convict on Article I but acquit on Article II. Trump remained in office for the remainder of his term; however, he was impeached for a second time in 2021 following the January 6 United States Capitol attack, making him the first U.S. president in history to be impeached twice. The Senate again acquitted Trump in February 2021, after he had already left office.

Trump's Case and My Thought

On June 16, 2015, Real Estate Developer Trump formally announced his Presidency Candidacy. Due to his candidacy, the media's obsession with dehumanizing him escalated. The dehumanization backfired and spread his popularity, especially in the South. Most Trump supporters viewed him as a Saver of the USA.

Trump's nationalistic campaign, which promised to "Make America Great Again" and opposed political correctness, illegal immigration, Banning Muslims and repealing many United States free-trade agreements, received extensive free media coverage worth billions of dollars free ad due to his comments that shook the 70-year-old political, economic, and military establishment. Of course, the establishment was nervous when Obama was running for the presidency, but after the election, he quickly became the establishment's puppet.

But, Trump will not be like Obama because he comes from a third-generation wealthy family and has all his life dealing with the high-end people in NYC and the world. He is also a real estate developer. That makes it difficult to convert him into a puppy, which is really terrifying for the establishment.

However, I have been pro-Trump since 2015, but I may not support him in the 2024 election. The reason I helped him and continuously wrote to Trump's FB until 2019 is that I believe he is not a media-creation clown politician and not a corrupt establishment "War Monger" for the trillion-dollar military industry and oil.

As I lived in NYC for a couple of decades, I heard a lot about him and met him a couple of times, once at the Jacob K. Javits Convention Center and another time at 58 ST.

As a New Yorker, I heard why most young kids used to hate him. The famous jealousy was that assumably Trump had sex with all the beautiful girls in the world because he partially owned "Beauty Pageants." As we all know, most young guys dream of having sex with beautiful girls. The second jealousy was "he is not worth what he says he is worth."

The case is all about second jealousy: " He is not worth what he says he is worth," with a political motive to prevent him from running in 2024. I found this case interesting. They accused him of "Fraud."

Technically, it could be a fraud case because there is a "Tax-related issue" involved if the financial statement and tax assessment have a discrepancy. As a property owner, he can say that whatever his property value is, it is up to him. If he can say a one-dollar apple is worth a billion dollars, he can say it, but tax authorities may assess his taxes based on what he is saying. "One dollar apple, a billion dollar tax assessment," nearly a quarter million dollar taxes.

The bottom line, all types of interest groups will try to destroy Trump by all means necessary, from bureaucratic to financial establishments. However, establishments have yet to realize that the USA is already exposed to the world. The sweet old days are over because, during the 1940s, hardcore defenders of the USA almost all died, and few are in feeble age. It is a wake-up call, not threatening with Nuke and sanction.

Donald Trump's Sexual Misconduct Allegations

False allegations have become a pervasive issue in the United States. According to a national survey sponsored by the Center for Prosecutor Integrity, 8% of Americans, or 20.4 million adults, have reported being falsely accused of sexual assault, domestic violence, or child abuse.

These false accusations can result in the loss of family ties, social stigmatization, impairment of career opportunities, mental health problems, and even wrongful convictions. Shockingly, nearly 2,000 Americans have been wrongfully convicted of a crime due to false allegations or perjury since 1989. False accusations and perjury have been found to be common contributors to wrongful convictions in cases involving child sex abuse and sexual assault.

Historically, false accusations of rape made by white women against African American men often resulted in wrongful convictions and led to extrajudicial acts of violence such as lynching. Causes of false accusations of rape fall into two categories: deliberate deception (lies) and non-deliberate deception such as false memories, facilitated communication, and "do not know."

As a matter of fact, an accuser may have several motivations behind to claim they have been raped falsely. These motivations can include financial gain, revenge, sympathy, attention, disturbed mental state, relabeling, or regret.

False memories can also contribute to false accusations of rape or sexual assault. It is essential to understand the complexity of these issues before drawing any conclusion. Scientifical study showed that helping behavior can be influenced by something as simple as touch that touching someone's arm or shoulder for just a couple of minutes while asking for a favor can significantly increase their compliance. This non-verbal contact may seem trivial, but it can have a big impact. However, this touches a revenge lady who can interpret it as sexual harassment. Of course, men are weaker toward pretty women that does not mean a sexual assault.

At a glance, Donald Trump, the President of the United States from 2017 to 2021, has been accused of rape, sexual assault, and sexual harassment, including nonconsensual kissing and groping, by at least 25 women, which might have happened from 1970 to the 2020s. His opponent intended to capitalize on them to humiliate and character assassinate him.

Litigation reflects his ex-wife Ivana's rape false claim

during their 1990 divorce case. She later withdrew. Jill Harth, a businesswoman's 1997 lawsuit alleging breach of contract and sexual harassment. She settled the former claim and withdrew the latter, a former Apprentice contestant Summer Zervos's claim of sexual misconduct, followed by a 2017 defamation lawsuit after Trump accused her of lying. She withdrew her defamation case in 2021.

In June 2019, writer E. Jean Carroll alleged in New York magazine that Trump raped her in a department store dressing room in 1995 or 1996. The magazine said two friends of Carroll confirmed that Carroll had previously confided in them in regard to the incident. Trump called the allegation fiction and denied ever meeting Carroll, although New York had published a photo of Trump and Carroll together in 1987.

On May 9, 2023, a New York jury in a civil case found Trump liable for sexual abuse and defamation against Carroll but found him not liable for rape by the New York state definition.

They awarded Carroll $5 million in damages. It was ruled that Trump had forcibly and nonconsensually penetrated Carroll's vagina but did so with his fingers, while New York state's definition at the time defined rape as solely nonconsensual penetration of the vagina by a penis.

In July, Judge Kaplan clarified that the jury had found that

Trump had raped Carroll according to the standard definition of the word. A September 2023 partial summary judgment again found Trump liable for defaming Carroll. On January 26, 2024, Trump was ordered to pay Carroll an additional $83.3 million in damages.

Two of the allegations by Ivana Trump and Jill Harth became public before Trump's candidacy for President. Still, the rest arose after a 2005 audio recording was leaked during the 2016 presidential campaign. Trump was recorded bragging that a celebrity like himself "can do anything" to women, including "just start kissing them ... I do not even wait" and "grab 'em by the pussy."

Trump subsequently characterized those comments as "locker room talk" and denied actually behaving that way toward women, and he also apologized for the crude language. Many of his accusers stated that Trump's denials provoked them into going public with their allegations. Another type of accusation was made, primarily after the audio recording surfaced, by several former Miss USA and Miss Teen USA contestants, who accused Trump of entering the dressing rooms of beauty pageant contestants.

Trump, who owned the Miss Universe franchise, which includes both pageants, was accused of going into dressing rooms in 1997, 2000, 2001, and 2006 while contestants were in various stages of undress. Trump had already referred to this practice during a 2005 interview on The Howard Stern Show, saying he could "get away with things like that" because he owned the beauty pageants in which the women and girls were competing.

In October 2019, the book All the President's Women: Donald Trump and the Making of a Predator[a] by Barry Levine and Monique El-Faizy was published, containing 43 additional allegations of sexual misconduct against Trump.

Trump has denied all the allegations against him, saying he has been the victim of media bias, conspiracies, and a political smear campaign. In October 2016, Trump publicly vowed to sue all the women who have made allegations of sexual misconduct against him, as well as The New York Times, for publishing the claims.

Why does the establishment hate Trump?

The toxic relationship between Donald Trump and the U.S. political establishment is a manifestation of a blind and unremitting hatred. From Trump's 91 criminal indictments to the predictivity of his re-election destroying the Republic Party, the political establishment has made their disdain for him clear.

But why does the establishment hate him so much? Simply put it this way, he is a threat to their hidden agenda, privilege, and, most of all, their power, to which they are addicted. Understanding this dynamic is vital to grasping what is happening in the United States and reflecting on ordinary American struggles and beliefs.

As gearing up for the upcoming U.S. presidential elections, the anti-elite message pushed by the Republican party has once again taken center stage. However, history has shown that despite running as Washington outsiders, Republican presidents have rarely governed that way.

The first Trump administration's failure, according to many Trump supporters, was its inability to break the power of the corruption-rooted bureaucracy and the liberal bias of the media and woke cultural institutions. Also, betrayal by Trump's establishment political appointees.

According to US Anti-elitism, a mandate for Leadership is

a blueprint for gutting the administrative state and directly attacking the "Woke-Industrial Complex." This battle will be fought well beyond the federal government, political establishment and the Ivy League.

All the left-wing elites who derive their power, prestige, and wealth from manipulating the federal budget will be in the crosshairs. As always, the messenger also sends the message. Will the next Trump administration finally deliver on the anti-elite promises he made during the campaign? Only time will tell.

The media and establishment may need to understand why Trump voters continue to support him despite all the media attacks, but perhaps it is not about Trump himself at all. Instead, his voters are drawn to the anti-elitism which he happens to represent. As the establishment continues to attack him, his supporters become more convinced that he is doing the right thing.

In fact, this loathing of the elites is becoming a defining political ideology of the USA, with voters expressing their deep dissatisfaction with the ruling class. So, instead of asking why Americans voted for Trump, the establishment needs to question why they rejoice so much in elite hatred.

America's New Saver Nikki Haley

At the end of every three years, the media begins searching for America's savers. By then, the presidential debate season was geared up, and the media's talk show hosts began building up noise to create America's Saver.

In my understanding, the media has two objectives: first, select a person who is easy to manipulate and appealing to lobbyists. Second, select a person who can charismatically warm up the crowd to put a roof on the fire. Rest assured, the media will create the brand to sell in the election market. The election market is scorching because the vast majority of election consumers are ignorant, so they are ready to jump on the fire.

What is America? According to the media branding, America is the "Land of Opportunity," "Land of Freedom," "American Dream," "American Exceptionalism," and "Democracy." The clown politicians rebrand them to incite the election consumers.

What is America's original principle? The Founding Fathers politically structured the nation as the USA, a Written Constitutional Republic, jealously safeguarding it with three branches of government so that a king-like government could not Centrally Govern the country like our current military dictators in the world.

Who is America's principal enemy? According to USA media, obviously, Islamic terrorists, Islamic Fundamentalists, and Islamic Extremists. The clown politicians heat the crowd with the bluff: "Bomb the hell out of them," eliminate them," "kill them all," and "smoke the hell out of them." The question is, do they know about Islam, Muslims and America's Muslim foreign relations and why Muslims first came to the USA? I am confident they do not know but love to hate Muslims.

Who is Nikki Haley? It is the media's creation of America's New Saver and counterproductive to the Media's enemy, Trump. The U.S. media is working toward making her the most significant American of all time.

Actually, who is she? Her parents immigrated to the United States from Amritsar, Punjab, India. Most of the Punjabi people shared painful memories of the 1947 partition when millions of Punjabis were slaughtered, and thousands of women were raped. Her hate for Muslims is justified.

Of course, her roots are also from the lower caste. She can relate to the Sountereners' lowlife people, which Hillary Clinton referred to as the "Basket of deplorables." She also bleached herself to look like more Caucasian.

In the South, Caucasian business is a hotcake. I was in the South for a few years. I learned it pretty well. In the South, only

Scapegoats is black people, and Muslims are devil worshippers. Muslim need to repent and accept Jesus as a saver, then they are fine. So many times, Southerners prayed on me to save me from Devil Worship.

In final words, I predicted in 2022 that the USA is heading to a "No-Return" if it does not change its course. Recently, I saw on "YouTube" that a well-educated Accountant predicted that the USA would collapse in 2034. The main enemy of the USA is the media. It destroyed the USA by spreading lies and sex, which corrupted the minds of people.

U.S. Primary 2024

The local, national and international news media bombarded the news that Former President Donald Trump secured the Republican nomination for the 2024 presidential election. His sweeping victories across the country expanded his delegate lead and ensured the nomination.

In fact, he has achieved the earliest date for any presumptive nominee in recent history. Democrat John Kerry held the previous record, who became the presumptive nominee on February 18, 2004, after Howard Dean dropped out of the race.

It was interesting to see him secure the Republican Party presidential nomination in the midst of dozens of ongoing legal battles.

Primary elections are an integral part of the voting process in the USA, allowing voters to indicate their preference for their party's candidate. The origins of primary elections can be traced back to the democratic movement in the United States, which aimed to take the power of candidate nomination from party leaders to the people.

While political parties control the method of nomination of candidates for office in the name of the party, primary elections are typically held for offices that have a rigid term, such as a president, governor, or member of a legislature. Other methods of selecting candidates include caucuses, internal selection by a party body such as a convention or party congress, direct nomination by the party leader, and nomination meetings.

The direct primary system, which allows party members to select their nominees for public office, has a long and complex history in the United States. While direct primaries became necessary at the state and local levels in the late 19th and early 20th centuries, presidential nominations continued to rely on state party conventions until 1972.

The Democratic party set up the McGovern-Fraser Commission in response to Hubert Humphrey's 1968 nomination without entering any state primaries, which rewrote the rules to emphasize primaries, and the Republicans followed suit.

The first primary elections were held in the Democratic Party in the South in the 1890s, starting in Louisiana in 1892. However, the primaries were run by party officials, making it easy to discriminate against black voters in the era of Jim Crow. It was not until 1944 that the U.S. Supreme Court declared the white primary unconstitutional in Smith v. Allwright.

Ironically, almost all blacks identify themselves as "Democrats". Both promoted the direct primary regular party leaders and progressive reformers like Robert M. La Follette of

Wisconsin, who led the successful fight for voter approval in a referendum in 1904.

Primary elections are an essential tool for party voters to express their likeness or dislikeness of a candidate to choose their preferred candidate for office.

The USA Foreign Policy

The U.S. Constitution laid out foreign policymaking responsibility to the executive and legislative branches. Congress can enact the regulation of foreign commerce, but it still divides between the two. The Constitution explicitly does not assign any of the government's components solely to foreign policy. The Constitution made the presidential chief of command, like a military and executive command. The president can declare war on foreign countries.

The USA's foreign policy evolved over the years based on the political decisions made by the president and Congress. In the beginning, the USA fought against imperialist colonial masters, the Europeans such as France, Spain, and Britain, for a hundred years in the name of "Freedom" and "Free Market Economy." Some of the colonial territories were fought, purchased, or politically admitted to the Union.

In the twentieth century, the USA politically fought against Soviet Communism for 70 years in the name of capitalism versus communism and atheism versus believers. However, President Harry Truman's doctrine has been the USA's focal foreign policy since 1945, known as the Cold War. The USA will not directly use the US military against the Soviet Union. Still, financial aid to support the economies and militaries wherever Soviet influence or movement is growing, mainly in Turkey and Greece. And in the twenty-first century, the so-called Islamic Terrorists for 20 years in Afghanistan and still ongoing.

Ideologically, these three USA foreign policies have three different political practices. The differences are No.1. Imperialism was a straightforward concept. The imperialist lured small kings with brick and cement to build big houses with a low-interest rate loan, provided a guaranteed defense treaty with the petty kings, and made the fort for the military. Over the years, they colonized it with a growing population and business.

No.2, Communism, in short, is a simple concept by Carl Marks, Lords, peasantry, slaves, and commoners are equal, and every employee will receive the same housing and payments. The economy can grow domestically by everyone working together as one community.

No. 3, Islamic Terrorists. Islamic Terrorists are CIA and ISI creation Taliban, Al-Qaida, and many other small groups. Saddam Hussein, Saddam Hussein's batheist (communist), was an American puppet during 1978-1990. He was an ideological communist and political and military with the USA to fight against Iran.

Historically, foreign policy in the Old World was based on water, land, and religious disputes. The Kings tried to solve the issues with the adversary by negotiating a treaty, marriage between king families, or war. But in the New World, the USA's foreign policy is not steady. It fluctuates as it sees fit.

Peace through strength

The Roman concept of "Peace through strength" was reaffirmed by the founding father of the U.S. He said in the 1793 State of the Union Address, "There is a rank due to the United States among nations which will be withheld, if not absolutely lost, by the reputation of weakness. If we desire to avoid insult, we must be able to repel it; if we desire to secure peace, one of the most powerful instruments of our rising prosperity, it must be known that we are at all times ready for war."

That was reassured by the famous President Ronald Regean. In 1980, Ronald Reagan used the phrase "Peace through strength" during his election bid against President Jimmy Carter. He accused him of being weak and indecisive leadership, which may have allowed the enemies to attack the United States soil and its allies.

However, President Ronald Reagan did not declare "War" on the Soviet Union or Iran. He did not shoot a bullet at Iran or the Soviet Union. He used Saddam Hussein to fight against Iran for eight long years, from 1980 to 1988, and mujahedeen against the Soviet Union. According to the authentic pieces of evidence and report, the United States actively supported the Iraqi war effort by supplying Saddam Hussein with billions of dollars of line of credit, providing U.S. military intelligence and advice to the Iraqi military, and closely monitoring third-country arms sales to Iraq to make sure that Iraq had the military weaponry necessary. The United States also provided strategic, operational advice to the Iraqis to better use their assets in combat. The CIA, including both CIA Director Casey and Deputy Director Gates, knew of, approved of, and assisted in the sale of non-U.S. origin military weapons, ammunition, and vehicles to Iraq. (NY Times, the State Department)

Also, President Ronald Reagan used the Afghan resistance fighters (mujahedeen) to repel the Soviet invasion as part of the larger Cold War strategy. After the Afghan victory, the U.S. stopped financially supporting the Afghans. This lack of financial support and withdrawal of the Soviet Union contributed to a power struggle between different tribes for control of Afghanistan, eventually culminating in a civil war. Some of the radical Mujahedeen fighters the CIA funded eventually formed the Taliban, gained control of Afghanistan, and allowed psychopaths like Osama bin Laden to establish a presence in Afghanistan.

President Ronald Reagan used Sunni Muslims against the Soviet Union to weaken the Soviet Union. He did not shoot a bullet at the Soviet Union or Iran to show U.S. military strength.

The clowns Sen. Lindsey Graham, Marco Rubio, Tim Scott, Susan Collins, Chris Coons, Richard Blumenthal, Ted Cruz,

Cory Booker, Dan Sullivan, and Katie Britt. Furthermore, Presidential Candidate Nikki Haley, those who shamelessly lie and spread hatred in the communities to fight Muslims, the situation will get severe, and the entire nation will pay the price if these clowns are not stopped.

September 11th And A War On Terror

My memory of September 11th. On September 11th, 2001, at 11 am, I had an appointment for LSAT Seminar at the World Trade Center. I set my alarm clock for 9:30 am. I slept after the Fajr Prayer. At about 9 am, my mother woke me up. She told me that her niece was on the phone telling her that a plane had hit the Twin Towers. I told her, Ma, "Do not worry, she might be watching a movie." "I have an appointment at 11 am in the World Trade Center".

My cell phone was under my pillow. I turned it on and saw a dozen text messages. My wife asked me, "Am I okay," I replied, what happened? "She replied, "NYC is under attack." I went to the bathroom, refreshed myself, and coffee made coffee in the kitchen. I took my coffee, sat on the sofa, and turned the T.V. on. I could not believe my eyes.

My mind began questioning, "Who did this?" KGB or Mossad. It cannot be a plane accident. It is a coordinated intelligence ring operation. Many people asked me why I thought of the KGB or Mossad. My answer is always the same. Common sense is the greatest gift God blesses us with. The KGB knew how the USA destroyed the Soviet Union by using Muslim Mujaheed in Afghanistan, Yemen, etc. Mr. Putin was the Head of the KGB. On his watch, the Soviets collapsed, and East and West Germany reunified. He will never forget this painful memory.

Mossad has an entirely different strategy than the KGB. Israel was created in 1948, then Israel has been fighting against many pockets of Palestinian resistance and a couple of Israel and Arabs wars. Israel won the Arabs war but failed to win the hearts of Muslim populations. There are more than fifty Muslim countries. Israel has been unable to gain the majority of the Muslim countries' support and recognition.

After 2000 the Palestinian uprising, Mossad may have thought that if a major attack on US soil, the USA would come and bomb the hell out of Palestinian terrorist groups, which may be an end game for Palestinians' violent resistance. And Saudi is an obstacle because the USA and Saudi made an unbreakable trade mutual agreement in 1945. Also, Saudi is a prime supporter of Palestine and may allow the US politicians to put financial sanctions on Saudi assets.

After a few days, my Army Officer called me to pick me up. He came to my house. I told him, "Sir, I cannot go to Army. I am sensing a river of blood. I do not trust this administration. The September 11th incident needed a thorough criminal investigation and deep analytical intelligence review before making any judgmental recommendation for an order."

He said, "You are a genius; the USA Army needs you." I

showed him a Quranic verse. "O, you who believe! If a rebellious, evil person comes to you with news, verify it, lest you harm people in ignorance, and afterward, you become regretful to what you have done" (49:6). He stood up and shouted at me, "You cannot bring religion in the USA Army code of conduct. Dismissed," He left. My mom got scared. I told her, "Ma, do not worry, it is a military talk.

In the region of Emilia-Romagna, in northern Italy, the War of the Bucket was fought in 1325 between Bologna and Modena. The bloodshed lasted over 300-year-long between Bologna and Modena just for a Bucket.

Modena won the Battle of Zappolino, the only battle of the war, and the Bucket remains in Modena to this day. The rumor surrounding the War of the Bucket is that the Modenese stole a bucket from a Bolognese well. However, that is primarily incorrect, as the Bucket was, according to correct accounts, taken as a trophy by the Modenese after the war. In fact, war was declared because Modena had captured the Bolognese castle of Monteveglio.

Like the War of the Bucket, George Bush's War on Terror fulfills his hidden agenda by fooling the vast majority of ignorant Americans by pretexting the September 11th attack. The objective was not to deter terrorism. But to get the pipeline through

Afghanistan and Iraqi oil. In the 1990s, George Bush was investing money in oil. His company lost a hundred billion dollars on the Iraq oil for food program.

There was no substantial evidence to believe that the Taliban and Saddam orchestrated the September 11th attack. The Taliban and Saddam had nothing to do with the September 11th horrific attack, but Osama Bin Laden proudly took credit. The media's hatred of Islam found an open field to shoot in the goal post "Islamic Terrorists" without any resistance and "Sex Politics." characterless Mayor Bloomberg pretext to humiliate practicing Muslims in NYC. The foolish hatred Bucket War needs to stop. President Joe Bidden showed authentic historical leadership.

Islamic Terrorists

"If anyone killed a person, not in retaliation of murder, or (and) to spread mischief in the land - it would be as if he killed all mankind, and if anyone saved a life, it would be as if he saved the life of all mankind. " **Alquran 5:32**

Going on for Islamic terrorists, Fox News and USA media's usual propaganda against the Muslim community upset me the most because they deliberately promoted lies about Muslims that poison the heads of ordinary people, complicating building social harmony. As ancient wisdom, "An ignorant is a poisonous snake; if it bites you, it will inject poison in you that will eventually kill you." So, walk away from the ignorant. An insignificant Muslim minority living in the USA was already struggling to cope with the post-September 11 situation. But by making Muslim scapegoats, ignorant media deliberately fueled hatred.

As a grandson of a Muslim League founding member and son of a late Muslim League leader, I felt my moral consciousness to pen down. Since the 7th C.E., Islam has been an ongoing political debate for Western Europeans.

Islam became one of the great Muslim civilizations, taking its peak with the Umar (R.D.) caliphate in the 7th Century century. In 711, Islamic Mujaheed, led by Tariq Ibn Ziyad, marched into Andalus. In seven years, they conquered the Iberian Peninsula

(Spain and Portugal). General Tariq decided to march in the Iberian because the Iberians verbally and physically abused newly reverted Muslims. Nowadays, Muslims are bullied daily by the media, politicians, and street rats in the USA.

Due to various factors, Islamic rule declined in Europe and ended in 1492 when the Crusaders conquered Granada. Western Europeans fought three crusades against Muslims with lies like the War on Terror.

When the USA was formed, the World had a different social, economic, religious, and political system. The political system was based on feudalism, The East India Companies, and the Church, except for the Islamic Khalifate.

Islam defined two types of responsibilities and accountabilities. No.1: Fard al-Ayn in Islamic law refers to individual responsibilities that must be performed by each Muslim, including five times prayer, charity, fasting, pilgrimage, etc. No. 2: Fard Kifaya is a communal responsibility in Islamic legal doctrine.

The media bombarded the nation with the lie that radical Islam was coming to establish the Khalifate. Khalifate is not an ideology. It is a governmental system created after three days of Prophet Muhammed (PBU) passing away. Prophet Muhammed (PBU) never instructed anyone to make a governmental system.

He was teaching people only Islam.

The US Constitution was the first complete written political Constitution in the World. It was a remarkably new idea in the World. The founding father, Lord George Washington, an Englishman first time in the World, chose to be a President, "became a president voluntarily and stepped down voluntarily." But then again, the media are creating chaos on the political stage in the expression of history-making.

The media made history by electing President Barack Hussein Obama. Before leaving office, President Barack Hussein Obama noted: "no blueprint for running a country" to Mr. Trump. But the founding fathers left a guiding principle, "The USA Constitution," to be followed by whoever assumed the Presidency. That is how media makes a political ignorant of a political icon.

The recent terrorist attacks in Europe and the USA are from lone actors: former colonials masters workers, interpreters, employees' grandchildren, and great-grandchildren. Those grandchildren and great-grandchildren had heard lots of imaginary fairytales about their grandfathers and great-grandfathers' masters. In reality, they are shocked because they live in a low-class society. Their bedtime stories and truth are not matched. What they have heard and experienced entirely different types of social behaviors is why they became terrorists, not because they are ideological

Islamic cadres.

My research showed that ideological Muslim activists did not commit most terrorist attacks. And their parents were not from traditional Muslim families. They are the product of US media propaganda and street bullies. End of the day, their grandparents or great-grandparents were named Muslim. They were human beings who did have bloodline from the Muslims. It is common sense that they were emotionally angry by seeing the daily basis humiliation of the Muslims in Europe and the USA.

We were born and raised in traditional Muslim families. We are always different from them because we are well informed in history, and we understand the social class system pretty well. Isolated terrorist attacks are expected because the root cause is an identity crisis and lack of integration with Western Society and the USA. It has nothing to do with Islam.

Taliban

The Taliban is a term the USA and International Media use to paint Islam as an evil religion. Frequently broadcast that the Taliban banned all the girls' schools and whipped a woman wearing a Burka. All the media outlets showed a Taliban beating a woman in public but never told the background story.

The root cause of the Taliban movement is a horrific incident, as far as I heard from some Afghani in NYC. Mullah

Omar was a prominent Mujaheed commander during the Soviet Union and Afghanistan war in 1979-1989. After the Soviet Union withdrew its military from Afghanistan, he returned to his village and taught kids the Quran. Between 1979-95, the lawlessness in Afghanistan created anarchy, loot, rape, murder, political assassination, robberies, burglaries, and widespread drug smuggling in the country.

One day, Mullah Omar was teaching the Quran to the kids. At that time, he heard a warlord cut a woman's vagina to see how a baby was born. Mullah Umar took his AK 47. He went to the one who committed that heinous crime. He killed that warlord in an execution-style; since then, his name has spread throughout the country, "Mullah Omar." A few former Islamic-minded Mujaheed advised Mullah Omar to form a political party to fight all the warlords and establish a government.

He refused to create a political party. He said, "My Talib (students) will deal with the Zalim (injustice). Since Talib spread from village to village, people started to believe Mullah Omar was ahead of the political government of Afghanistan. Mullah Omar repeatedly stated that he is not a politician or Islamic scholar. He is just fighting against Zalim (injustice).

When the Taliban negotiated a deal with Governor George Bush to rebuild Afghanistan's infrastructure, Governor George

Bush and the Taliban agreed. But Mullah Omar rejected paying any interest on the loan; that was the exact problem between George Bush and Mullah Omar. The interest issue on loans could have been solved by creating a financing mechanism, but the media was the mother of all problems.

The media bombarded the World with the Taliban's negative image that the Taliban beat women and banned girls' schools instead of the media reporting the whole story about the incidents. That created a wall between the Taliban and the USA. The USA was the strongest ally of the Mojaheedun; the Mujaheedun defeated a most considerable superpower that the USA was waiting for revenge for Vietnam's humiliation, but the media made the Taliban a friend to a foe.

Why did the Taliban trust Governor George Bush? Because his father was Ronald Reagan's Vice President. Ronald Reagan's administration directly, politically, financially, and militarily helped Mullah Omar from 1979 to 1989 to fight against the Soviet Union.

The Taliban issue could have been resolved in the late 1990s if the Media had not complicated the situation. Corrupt politicians' focal point is seeking media attention to become famous, unlike traditional politicians whose primary agenda is "national interest" and defending the nation and its people.

As a result, more than two trillion were wasted, and thousands of lives were sacrificed with lies. The Media is again complicating the political situation with the Taliban with their whimsical feelings. Their impulsive feelings are not guided by knowledge, wisdom, logic, condition, or expertise. At this time, the World has the opportunity to help the Taliban politically, financially, and technologically to put a full stop to the war in a half-century wartorn country.

Afghanistan Withdrawal

On July 8th, 2021, President Joe Biden said: "There's going to be no circumstance where you see people being lifted off the roof of an embassy of the United States from Afghanistan." He was referring to on March 29, 1973, the last U.S. military unit left Vietnam.

In fact, it was actually much worse. I saw videos of Afghans clinging to the outside of planes during takeoff, with many falling to their deaths. Afghans who were assisting the USA turned away and threw themselves on razor wire surrounding the airport rather than face torture at the hands of the Taliban,

Republican party accused the Taliban and the Biden administration of continuously violating the conditions of President Trump's agreement and did not hold them accountable.

The Biden administration had been warned that the Taliban would stop at nothing until they retook the country. Now, the Taliban is back in power. The decision of the Biden Administration to withdraw from Afghanistan was a historic, courageous decision that I have been asking for a long time.

America's Longest War:

What Went Wrong in Afghanistan? CNN asked.

I watched a CNN documentary in which top US

commanders from the war wrestled with mistakes and regrets to discover what went wrong. It was one of a kind. I never saw anything like that program. However, I watched Michael Moore's Fahrenheit 9/11 documentary film in 2004 with my wife in Kew Gardens, Queens, NYC.

Regarding the Afghanistan War, I have a completely different "Intelligence Analytical" assessment than a 100% conventional intelligence expert thought-through assessment. USA Conventional Intelligence gathering means " Copying and Pasting" on a piece of paper or Microsoft Word and receiving a weekly paycheck directly deposited to the personal account.

To me, it is less likely to be reliable and credible. Getting drunk and looking for virgin girls in Muslim countries will never give the correct assessment. To understand this, we can take an example: "Andrew Warren is a 6-foot-4 African American schooled in the martial arts. Steeped in Middle Eastern history, he was a convert to Islam who spoke six Arabic dialects. He was a natural to be the CIA's top man in Algiers". This guy was all about having sex with Muslim women, not gathering intelligence. He was a CIA top dog. How could you trust his opinion?

In spite of this, I opposed any war until a concrete "Intelligence Assessment was Produced." Of course, President Bush would not like it, and he had already made up his mind for wars, and all Americans want retaliatory action.

Indeed, what do you expect from Pokémon, Dragon Quest, Final Fantasy IX, Tony Hawk's Pro Skater, Chrono Cross players and Sadistic? Except for retaliation. None of them will understand that "Patience is key to success."

Before making any decision, these three things must be critically considered.

No. 1, what is the objective?

No.2, what would you like to do?

No.3 The risk and gain must be scrutinized and thoroughly assessed.

In my understanding, President Bush did not believe in the "Principle of deterrence, prevention and retribution." His political motive was to use his anger to invade Afghanistan for an oil pipeline and invade Iraq for oil, as he was an oil businessman.

I do not believe caveman Osama bin Laden orchestrated the 9/11 operation. A caveman cannot do it. There was no substantial evidence to link him to 9/11, except he took credit for it. That was obviously an intelligence ring operation. However, September 11 could have been a pretext to wipe out the entire Osama bin Laden network by injecting intelligence infiltration into the network that might have taken a couple of years, definitely not

20 years, thousands of civilians, military personal lives and more than two trillion dollars in debt.

In the end, boastful egoists and arrogant "War Monger" will never listen to the "word of wisdom." and sadistic will never understand the "Precious lives of human beings." A sadistic loves bloodshed and destruction and enjoys human suffering. Americans wanted war; they got more. Now what, where is the country heading? More video games war.

Biden Admin Has 'Undermined' Israel.

The Biden administration has 'undermined' Israel: Sen. Cruz (Fox News). The Truth Will Set You Free (John 8:32). These days, principles of ethical decision-making have become a challenge in the USA. The mainstream media has created a culture of promoting lies, hate, demonization, backbiting and slandering that discourages ordinary people from seeking truth and becoming productive citizens.

In my opinion, Fox News is a prime enemy of the USA and a great promoter of anti-Muslim propaganda. It frequently invokes the "USA was founded based on "The Judeo-Christian Tradition."

I will not argue in this about the root of "The Judeo-Christian Tradition" propaganda in the USA. But I can confidently say that the U.S. Constitution guarantees "Freedom of Religion." Also, I will not waste my time on fraud and pathological liar Sen. Ted Cruz, who is one of the vicious enemies of Muslims and Islam in the USA. A shameless liar who was born in Canada, not in the USA, but intended to be the US president. The Constitution states, "No Person except a natural born Citizen, or a Citizen of the United States, at the time of the Adoption of this Constitution, shall be eligible to the Office of President; neither shall any Person be eligible to that Office who shall not have attained to the Age of thirty-five Years, and been fourteen Years a Resident within the

United States." He thinks Americans are fools because his father came to the USA by fooling the U.S. border guard and married his mother by flattering.

Let us know about the historic relationship between the USA and Israel. In the beginning, the USA's support for Jews was hardly known to any Americans. Jews barely existed in the U.S. Jews came to be known to Americans through Louis Brandeis, the Federation of American Zionists, in 1912. Also by the Provisional Executive Committee for General Zionist Affairs in 1914.

President Wilson showed sympathy for the plight of Jews in Europe. He favored the Zionist view of "A Hewish Homeland" " On March 2, 1919, he said, "I am persuaded that the Allied nations with the fullest concurrence of our Government and people are agreed that in Palestine shall be laid the foundation of a future Jewish commonwealth." On April 16, 1919, the U.S. government's "expressed acquiescence" in the Balfour Declaration. On September 21, 1922, the U.S. Congress passed the Lodge-Fish resolution, the first joint resolution stating its support for "the establishment in Palestine of a National Home for the Jewish People." On the same day, the Mandate of Palestine was approved by the Council of the League of Nations.

During World War II, U.S. foreign policy often changed due to the demand to join the war. The Zionist movement made a fundamental change from the original Zionist policy. In May 1942, it stated its intention at the Biltmore Conference to establish a "Jewish National Home" in Palestine that replaced with " Jewish Commonwealth Palestine" like other nations, in cooperation with the United States, not Britain.

In 1944, U.S. Congress tried twice to pass the resolutions declaring U.S. government support for the establishment of a "Jewish Commonwealth" in Palestine, which the Departments of War and State objected to due to wartime considerations and Muslim opposition.

The resolutions were permanently dropped. However, the British created Israel in 1948, and the USA recognized it. There was no American involvement in the creation of Israel, as Fox News tried to sell.

Antisemitism Exposed (Fox News)

What is Semitism? I bet 99.9 % of people do not know what it is. But the emotional fools will vehemently defend Semitism. Let us know what anti-Semitism is. The 'Semitic' meant linguistic groups, not particularly a race. The term is a contradiction with the interpretation because there are many speakers of Semitic languages, such as Arabs, Ethiopians, and Arameans, who are not the subject of antisemitic prejudices. However, there are many Jews also who do not speak Hebrew, a Semitic language. Therefore, 'anti-semitism' should not be considered as prejudice against only Hebrew-speaking Jewish people. Some have spoken the Yiddish language of the Jewish people.

According to Islam, followers of these books, the Torah (given to Moses), the Gospel (given to Jesus), the Psalms (given to David), and the Scrolls (given to Abraham) are considered Ahl al-kitab (People of the book) the Latinization is Semitic.

What Fox News meant by anti-semitism: Antisemitism is hostility to, prejudice towards, or discrimination against Jewish people, but all Jews do not speak Hebrew. Fox News is a sworn enemy of Muslims and Islam. It systematically spread hatred against Muslims and Islam.

Fox News tends to demonstrate a pro-Christian and Jewish broadcast. For nearly 30 years, I have been watching "FoxNews."

I saw no educational program about Christianity or Jews. It manufactures lies, recruits Muslim and Islam hatred and tries to make them American icons or USA savers. Fox News is a serious threat to the existence of the USA.

I can confidently say that none of the Fox News anchors or hosts understand what they are talking about because they are fundamentally ignorant and mindlessly hateful toward Muslims and Islam.

Common sense tells us that when we were born, we knew nothing. The first word we learn is Ma, and the second word we learn is Ba. From thereon, our learning process begins. When our brain starts learning how to think, we begin to have the intellectual capacity to distinguish between right and wrong. It is clear to me that Fox News is braindead or blind to hate. And the nation is at stake.

The War is between two entities, the State of Israel and an organized group, Hamas. Israeli Jewish believe Israel is their ancient land, and Hamas believes Israeli Jews are occupiers. It has nothing to do with Anti-Semitism. People are emotionally and angrily supporting Palestine due to Israeli excessive bombardment and civilian casualties.

The Fox News iconic clown Nikki Haley said, "Kill them all." She has a profound identity crisis. She bleached too much to look like Caucasian. Now, she is coming to defend the Semitic people. What a clown show staged by Fox News.

Nikki Haley, the U.S. President

The generation born and raised in the "illusion of choice" has no basic understanding of the reality of life but is highly involved in political decision-making on Facebook, where six media companies control the minds of 90% of Americans who make decisions based on media hype and have zero understanding of the foundation of basics.

The U.S. media Revenue is projected to reach US$486.90bn in 2023. The market's largest segment is T.V. and video, with a market volume of US$275.70 bn in 2023.

The famous saying, "Whoever controls the media controls the minds of America." However, I read an article in the Washington Post: "Media coverage of the 2016 campaign was disastrous. Now's the last chance to get 2020 right." Of course, all the polls and so-called Political Pundits were wrong, but I was 100% correct. My prediction was that Mr. Trump would win the 2016 election, and the 2020 media would fiercely try to knock him out.

Let us compare Islam and America's politics:

Siasa (Politics): Islam and America have a 360-degree opposite understanding of politics. Islam understands politics as political principles that resolve domestic and foreign disputes politically instead of bloodshed and govern the country peacefully. As the Quran instructed, "Invite to the way of your Lord with wisdom and fair preaching and argue with them with that which is best" (16:125).

To be an Islamic politician, one must have high moral and ethical standards and social acceptance. Without social acceptance, people will never respect or listen to a politician. To politically control people, they must admire the politician.

American media understand politics as political activities such as rhetoric, bluff and often dishonesty, backbiting, slandering, and slumdog quarrel. To me, it is a pure clown show; they can not take care of their family but wish to solve 331 million people's issues. Top of that complex foreign policy. A ridiculous joke.

As I predicted media will try to create an America's saver, Nikki Haley. According to the survey conducted by Marquette Law School, Trump has an advantage of 52% to 48% over Biden among registered voters, while DeSantis holds a 51% to 49% advantage in a head-to-head matchup with the president. And Haley, who also previously served as governor of South Carolina, holds a 55% to 45% edge over Biden, the largest lead among

Republican candidates. (Fox News) but their plan did not work; she was defeated in the primary election landslide.

Muslim and American Relationship

In the late 40s, as the son of a former Pakistan Muslim League leader and East Pakistan regional minister, I heard from my father's coffee table conversation that Muslim leaders expressed their willingness to build a good relationship with the USA for concrete reasons. No.1, the USA is a new country thousands of miles away from Pakistan, and the Saudi King had a historical mutual agreement with the USA in 1945. The USA is technologically advanced, politically stable, and religiously tolerant.

After colonialism ended, the newly formed Muslim countries could not fight against the "Godless Superpower Soviet Union." That is why they needed a religious-friendly country. The US Constitution guarantees "Freedom of Religion" that Muslims can freely practice their religion "Islam" without fearing converting to Christianity. History suggests Pakistan was created in the name of Muslim nationalism.

No.2, New Muslim Independent countries needed to learn money management. After nearly three hundred years of fighting against colonial powers, Muslims needed to learn how to build their nations. There was no alternative except two choices: the USA or the Soviet Union.

No.3, after dissolving the "East India Companies," the

trade had become a challenge; that is why creating a trade currency was the most critical issue. Gold and silver were not realistic solutions for Pakistan because of overpopulation and the necessity to modernize the military and governmental system and industrialize the nation, which required lots of money that Pakistan did not have.

Afghanistan also was one of the Muslim countries that followed the Muslim leaders in the late 1940s to build a relationship with the USA.

As far as I know, Muslim countries did not support the USA in lecturing them on their domestic and religious issue. Instead, they wanted a friendlier Muslim and less hostile than colonialists. They fought against colonial powers to preserve their religious tenets that the US media and politicians did not understand.

And also, Muslims are so divided that it is humanly impossible to unite them. As a practical understanding, Pakistan can be used as an example. Pakistan was created in the name of Muslim nationalism within 23 years. Pakistan gave birth to another nationalist Bengali who hated Pakistan viciously.

In 1906, the Muslim League was founded in Dhaka, and the Muslim League created Pakistan on August 14, 1947. However, Pakistan is a curse to Bengalis, whereas East Bengal was the original founder of Pakistan. It is a learning key point; Bengalis were thousands of years Hindu's slaves (Proza). Muslims fought to liberate them from Hindu petty Raja and Zamindars' slavery but within 23 years of Pakistan's history. They hated Pakistan and Muslims. They fought to be Bengali.

During the 1971 war between India and Pakistan, my father was the "Peace Committee's Standing Committee Chairman." He witnessed disunity tremendously among Muslims, Bengalis, and Pakistanis. That is why he let the Indian Army take over East Pakistan.

At the 1971 war in East Pakistan, all the Pro-Pakistani political party leaders elected my father as the "Peace Committee's Standing Committee Chairman." On the night of December 13th, 1971, my father deeply thought about all the scenarios:

1. Bengal was off and on with India for thousands of years.
2. Pakistan was created based on Muslim nationalism; nearly 95% do not know Allah and have a core belief in monotheism.
3. There are dozens of Muslim sects; it is impossible to unite them under Muslim nationalism.
4. There was growing regional nationalism.
5. There were mushrooming political ideologies.
6. There were substantially numbered people alarming poor

because of two hundred years of Hindu zamindar slavery.

After carefully thinking about all the factors in the end, he made up his mind. Early in the morning of December 14th, 1971, he telegrammed Peace Committee Presidents and Secretaries in 1971 in 64 thousand villages, 5 thousand unions, 64 Mohokuma, 16 districts, and four divisions dated December 14th, 1971. It clearly said," I have a great feeling, by discussing with Sha Azziz, that "by overseeing eight months war, and drunk Yaha Khan leadership, I am certain to a belief that Indian military will march into Dhaka. If they march into Dhaka, there must be no street resistance, violence, or guerrilla war tactics. We swear on the Quran to protect and secure our people's safety in order to preserve our sovereignty. We failed to defend the sovereignty but the safety of the people on our hands."

This copy of the telegram was in my father's file until his death. I have read it more than a hundred times, but my father told me not to tell anyone. His telegram clearly indicates that he accepted India's occupation. However, on December 16th, 1971, the Peace Committee burned all the war records, and Ms. Indira Ghandi burned all the War Records in 1972. Also, Bangladesh President Sheikh Mujibur Rahman, father of Bangladeshi Bengali, burnt and banned all the newspapers except four in 1974.

The mainstream culture in Muslim countries is criminality,

fraudulent activities, rape, murder, robberies, burglaries, prostitution, and bribery. The subculture is religious ignorance divided into hundreds of groups. They hate each other for nothing, only for minor differences of opinion. It is impossible to find any reliable information from Muslims in Afghanistan, Bangladesh, and Pakistan.

They can give the wrong information for various factors such as revenge, jealousy, hatred, land, money, etc. And also, their tribal affiliations play a critical role in providing information. In the Muslim community, for thousands of years, there have been two sworn enemies, Shia and Sunni. The War on Terror was the dumbest idea ever the World witnessed.

The smartest thing to do to play foreign policy with the Muslim countries is never to use force. Whoever they make their head of the state, deal with them diplomatically. Never use the money and military. The corrupt government will steal the funds. If you use the military, the religious elements will wage an indefinite Jihad (struggling against the enemy with the weapon).

The USA Is the World Leader

In the middle of the 1940s, Western European and Muslim leaders crowned the USA as the world leader. As the son of a late Muslim League leader, I am fully aware of why Muslims favored the USA over the Soviet Union. Muslims are believers in Monotheism, and the Soviet Union was a Godless atheist, ideologically communist country. Contrary to the Western Europeans and Japan, Western Europe and Japan were bowing down to the USA under its military might. During the 2nd World War, the USA defeated Japan. The USA liberated Western Europeans from German military might, whereas Muslims fought against colonial powers for nearly three hundred years for their religious identity.

The USA planned to create an International Organization (U.N.), A secret wartime meeting between President Franklin D. Roosevelt and King Abdul Aziz ibn Saud on February 14th, 1945, in a U.S. Navy destroyer in the Suez Canal. Historically, it was the first time a U.S. president met with a Saudi King and laid a foundation for U.S.-Saudi relations that would continue for generations to come. That specific reason is that after independence from colonial powers, most Muslim countries leaned toward the USA.

Most people may not understand why the Saudi and USA

relationship was vital for the Muslims' support for the USA. Saudi has two crucial Muslim holy sites in its custody that gave Muslims a soft corner for the Saudi Government. And Saudi silently enjoys the Sunni Muslims' leadership.

Historically, there was no hostility between the USA and Muslims. Mistrust grew after the British created Israel in 1948 between Muslims and the USA. The Zionists had the most influential lobbyist group in the USA. The USA and Zionists built an unbreakable relationship with Israel, and the US media systematically dehumanized the Muslims. That complicated the USA and Muslims' political relationship.

The USA is a founding member of the United Nations, World Bank, International Monetary Fund, Organization of American States, and NATO. The USA is also a permanent member of the United Nations Security Council. More than forty Sunni Muslim countries unconditionally backed the USA between 1945 to 1970.

The United States was a highly technologically developed country and scored high in economic performance measures, two factors that appealed to the Muslims' newly independent countries.

However, since the U.N.'s founding in 1945, the organization's mission and work have changed from the original "To maintain international peace and security" to "Mutual

Respect," which was amended three times in 1963, 1965, and 1973.

Third World War

About a decade ago, some so-called political analysts and pundits predicted that an inexperienced and impulsive President, Donald Trump, would take the world into World War III.

Now, according to U.S. media, we are under a most experienced foreign policy expert, President Bidden, inching to an outbreak of so-called WW III.

For some people, experiencing WWIII is adventurous because there were hundreds of imaginary movies and video games have been made about it. Some are thrilled to make it a lifetime experience. On the other hand, the sadistic are impatiently waiting to see the mass-scale human suffering to satisfy their hunger for sadistic pleasure that would be hellaciously fun to them.

However, the fact is that Muslims never fought any W.W. Historically, Muslims fought crusades and Muslim-to-Muslim conflicts, not WWs. The WWs are European and USA brands of war, not Muslim.

In a recent fundraising leaked email, President Trump grieved over recent Wars, stated: "It truly breaks my heart to see Crooked Joe—the weakest and most incompetent president in history—ruin our country as he pushes America to the brink of World War III."

The ongoing wars between Russia and Ukraine, Israel, and Hamas. There are 32 countries currently at war among 193 UN Member States, including Russia and Ukraine are at war. Afghanistan, Ethiopia, Iraq, Yemen, Syria, Somalia, Libya, the Central African Republic, the Democratic Republic of Congo, Myanmar, Colombia, and Mali are currently in civil wars. Mexico is at war with the drug cartels in the country.

The American Psychological Association conducted a survey almost immediately after Russia invaded Ukraine last year to see the minds of Americans regarding WWIII, which found that nearly 7 in 10 Americans believed "that we are at the beginning stages of World War III." However, during his campaign, President Trump bragged that he was the "only one that will prevent World War III."

How will he prevent the wars? It is just the beginning of the wars, and the USA is about to declare bankruptcy, where the debt is piling up the burden of interest obligation.

He cannot bribe them, and the wars will turn into revenge wars, which no one will be able to stop. That was why, since 2002, I have been warning not to get into endless war. Muslims fought against colonialists for nearly 300 years.

Historic lesson: East India Companies created Hindu Raja and Zamindars and bureaucrats to fight against Muslims in the

Indian Subcontinent.

In the USA, everyone believes the USA has nukes and sanctions power that will get them scared. I said, "No". Muslim countries are not Japan. They can fight by eating leaves. Every three guys can create a group by taking Quranic verses out of context. The world needs a wise leader who sincerely believes in sustainable peace, not war.

Conclusion

"Messenger of Allah (ﷺ) said: "O 'Abdur-Rahman! Do not ask for a leadership position, for if you receive it due to asking, you will be left alone with it, and if you receive it without asking, you will be aided in it. And if you take an oath and you see that something else is better than it, then do what is better and make an atonement for your oath." **(at-Tirmidhi 1529)**

In conclusion, the USA is in a deep constitutional and political crisis, but no one seems concerned. The media is busy with concepts of history-making by dictating race politics and sexual politics.

In reality, history is made by itself. No one intends to make any history. History-making is a gradual process, not designed to be made.

I was recently watching YouTube. There has been too much nonsense on YouTube. I think most politicians take their policy materials from the media and social media instead of knowledge, facts and logical reasoning. Of course, the Constitution gave the right to "freedom of speech."

The speech does not necessarily mean expressing whimsical, vulgar words. Speech means the intellectual ability to express thoughts or feel articulate sound. The entire nation is filled with insanity and whimsical opinionists.

I live in a country where 70% of the working class cannot pay taxes. But, the government has the burden of a budget of S4.79 trillion as of today. No one seems to bother to know where the money will come from. A nation does not have the savings to bear the burden of preparing for a national emergency and cannot help its citizens in a tough time except by printing bills in the name of public debt—a straight 20-year budget deficit. The US citizens are burdened with a foreign debt of $6.81 trillion and the U.S. national debt of about $34.39 trillion as of March 1, 2024, by an estimated U.S. population of 336 million. This yields a national debt per capita of more than $102,000. A chronic trade deficit. Forty million Americans receive food stamps. 62.9 percent of households have a mortgage.

The family structure no longer exists. Individualism is the new social standard in the USA. Obviously, most people cannot fulfill their basic needs independently during emergencies, such as food, shelter, and water. It is seriously a nightmare, but the media's focal issue is sex. The media sells sex and promotes sex for vicious enmity toward religious values. The main attack on Islamic terrorists and promoting democracy cause substantial damage to its domestic and foreign policy.

The USA needs leadership. As the grandson of a Muslim

League founding member and son of a late Muslim League leader, I understand leadership precisely. I always tried not to get involved with politics. I usually wanted to live my life free and independent. Conversely, I tried to build relationships with the low-class and upscale to understand their differences.

I always failed. Psychologically and socially, both are very different in interaction and understanding; linguistic usages are also very different from each other. The socially upscale people look down on socially disadvantaged people. The socially disadvantaged people are always envious, jealous, and angry at the upscale people. But Islam creates mental peace in all social levels of the human being by teaching everyone Al-Qadar (Predestination).

Non-Muslim socially disadvantageous people, until the end of time, blame upscale for their misfortune. The middle class falls into three categories: upper-middle class, middle-class, and lower-middle class. The middle class is known as a buffer zone because it has economic interaction on both sides of the aisle. They are also known as the silent group. On top of that, humans have been religiously divided for thousands of years.

Karl Marx thought he could make everyone socially and economically equal and categorize religion as opium using governing capacity. Vladimir Lenin believed in Karl Marx's theory, executed landlords and industrialists, redistributed land among the peasantry, nationalized banks and large-scale industry, and banned all religious practices in 1990 after 70 years of Lenin's revolution were proven wrong. More Russians are heading in a spiritual direction.

The founding fathers used the phrase "all men are created equal" to appease men and unite them to fight against British imperialism. Literally, they did not mean that "all men are created equal"; the Constitution is evidence of this. If they believed in it, they would have made it constitutional: "All men are created equal."

Historically, all the Kings used to say, "Everyone is Equal under Law." All the rulers used this "Everyone is Equal under the Law" phrase to show that they treated their subjects impartially.

Scientifically, we know that it is impossible to believe that "all men are created equal." We are intellectually, physically, socially, economically, and emotionally different from each other. Theoretically, there are sixteen types of human personality, but we all agree on the "Justice" and "human dignity" that we all deserve.

Reality check: the harsh truth is that every human being deserves justice served. Simultaneously, every human being lies and denies the truth. Finding out the truth requires an investigation, which is time-consuming and expensive.

In the world, every government's moral obligation is to investigate every citizen's complaint, which is impossible. That was why the government took legal responsibility to deter and prevent only index crimes such as murder, rape, burglary, robbery, theft, fraud, and treason for thousands of years and categorized them as felonies.

As the USA constitution preamble states, a "tranquil society" is one in which good parenting can deter and prevent minor criminality in society, ensuring a peaceful society. Name of democracy electing random people who do not understand the core concept of governance that will not eliminate prejudices, racial hatred, or economic equality.

Authentic leadership is good parenting, which is the most challenging thing to do—not lying eloquently to fool the ignorant, known as socially disadvantageous people, for vote bank. Genuine leaders such as George Washington, Abraham Lincoln, Ronald Reagan, Nelson Mandela, Karamchand Gandhi, etc., stand for truth and justice. They genuinely understood the situation and made decisions based on their understanding. They also knew their consequences. They were willing to sacrifice. Their intention was not to be history-making but for the cause they believed in. A just cause.

References

1. K. M. Kostyal, John M. Thompson, William R Gray. Who's Who in American History, Leaders, Visionaries, and Icons who shaped our nation, National Geographic, Washington, D.C

2. al-Munajjid, S. M. S. (2001, April 16). *The Creation of Man.* Retrieved 2021, from https://islamqa.info/en/answers/13286/the-creation-of-man.

3. Kennedy, L. (2018, October 18). *How FDR Charmed a Saudi King and Won U.S. Access to Oil.* Retrieved 2021, from https://www.history.com/news/fdr-saudi-arabia-king-oil.

4. Malenaph. (n.d.). *World history.* Retrieved 2021, from https://www.timetoast.com/timelines/enlightenment-67a06c42-af61-45ac-bf7e-f16d5c82d98c.

5. National Constitution Centre. (n.d.). *Article I - Legislative Branch.* Retrieved 2021, from https://constitutioncenter.org/interactive-constitution/article/article-i.

6. National Women's History Museum. (21AD). *"At Last" The Suffragist.* 19th Amendment - History of U.S. Woman's Suffrage. Retrieved 2021, from http://www.crusadeforthevote.org/19th-amendment.

7. Office of the Historian. (n.d.). *Historical Documents*. Retrieved 2021, from https://history.state.gov/historicaldocuments.

8. *Sahih Bukhari: Book of "Freeing Slaves."* (n.d.). Retrieved 2021, from Sahih Bukhari: Book of "Freeing Slaves."

9. Taylor, A. (2015, January 27). *The first time a U.S. president met a Saudi King*. Retrieved 2021, from https://www.washingtonpost.com/news/worldviews/wp/2015/01/27/the-first-time-a-u-s-president-met-a-saudi-king/.

10. United Nations. (n.d.). *United Nations Charter*. Retrieved 2021, from https://www.un.org/en/about-us/un-charter.

11. Wharton Business Daily. (2020, September 8). *Getting the Job Done: How Immigrants Expand the U.S. Economy*. Retrieved 2021, from https://knowledge.wharton.upenn.edu/article/how-immigrants-expand-the-u-s-economy/.

12. The World Reporter. (2011). *1971 India Pakistan War Role of Russia*. Retrieved 2021, from https://www.theworldreporter.com/2011/10/1971-india-pakistan-war-role-of-russia.html.

13. https://www.migrationpolicy.org/

14. https://www.pewresearch.org/short-reads/2021/04/13/key-facts-about-the-changing-u-s-unauthorized-immigrant-

population/

15. Creation of Man in Islam - Islam Question & Answer. https://islamqa.info/en/answers/13286/creation-of-man-in-islam

16. https://www.trumpreporter.net/how-do-i-contact-donald-trump/

17. https://www.foxnews.com/us/north-korean-defector-ivy-league-nuts

18. https://abcnews.go.com/Politics/list-trumps-accusers-allegations-sexual-misconduct/story?id=51956410

19. https://www.theguardian.com/us-news/2016/nov/04/donald-trump-teenage-rape-accusations-lawsuit-dropped

20. https://lawandcrime.com/high-profile/exclusive-inside-the-donald-trump-sexual-assault-lawsuit/

About The Author

Shahinul Islam Khalisdar, EA, MST, is the grandson of a Muslim League founding member and son of a late Muslim League leader by profession, a Tax Advisor. He was born in Sylhet, Bangladesh. He has been living in the USA for a very long time. He has witnessed the political climate and media propaganda all his life. Due to anti-Muslim sentiment skyrocketing globally, some people asked him to pen down as a grandson and son of a Muslim League leader.

Bengali Wins Freedom is Shahinul Islam Khalisdar's fourth book, renamed 2nd Book *Reluctant Fathers*, and the first book in Bangladeshi political science. He aims to bring the truth because Bangladeshi media systematically brainwashed Bangladeshi Bengali for the last 30 years. And portrayed Muslims as rapists, murderers, and foreign culture importers.

His main aim is to write a comprehensive book based on his personal experiences, which are straightforward and stick with the truth, facts, policy, and expert opinions. He has also written on LinkedIn, President Trump's Facebook page, Prime Minister Narendra Modi, Imran Khan, and Sheikh Hasina's son, Sajeeb Wazed. Behind the scenes, he advised dozens of high-profile Muslim country leaders from 1995 to 2006 in NYC on critical political issues and foreign policy.

173